MW01231986

The Evolution of Happiness

in

Diverse Religions and Schools of Psychology

GERALD JEROME JORDAN
Th.D.

Omonomany

Memphis

Published by

Omonomany

5050 Poplar Avenue, Suite 1510

Memphis, TN 38157

(901) 374-9027 • Fax (901) 374-0508

Email jimweeks12@msn.com

www.omonomany.com

LCCN 2005937719

ISBN-10:   1-59096-004-1

ISBN-13:   978-1-59096-004-2

123456789

Printed in the United States of America

Table of Contents

Introduction

It has become increasingly more difficult to form a generally accepted concept of mental health and happiness. There are now so many schools of thought concerning mental health, and treatment approaches to improve mental well-being, that a reader can become quickly lost in the maze of conflicting theories. Different cultures and religions have differing ideas about what constitutes a sane and productive member of society. Different subgroups within a culture may have totally divergent ideas concerning these same concepts.

However, through virtually all of these conflicting messages, there is a recurring and persistent realization that humans need something that provides them with more than a meaningless life of eating, sleeping, reproducing and dying. Even cultures denying God have substituted the state, or subjugation of individual needs, to the welfare of all humans, as something to which an individual can dedicate his or her life and reach beyond his or her small existence. In both cases we are stating that a life lived only for the moment and only for an individual's momentary pleasure is a life that is wasted and forlorn. The present work is an analysis of how these themes play out both in different religions and different schools of psychology.

Three different major religions will be studied to analyze similarities of view concerning what constitutes mental health and a productive member of the religious community: Christianity, Buddhism, and Hinduism. While each of these religions have many identifiable subgroups, this work will concentrate on the major tenants of the religion generally accepted by each of the subgroups. Hinduism and Buddhism were chosen because they represent religious concepts that are quite removed from Western tradition and Christianity. If these religions also contain similar concepts of mental health, ethics and morality; the viability – truth – of such concepts should be given more weight.

Three major schools of thought in psychology and their accompanying concepts of mental health, mental illness, and treatment for mental disorders will be reviewed: experimental psychology, psychoanalysis, and behavior therapy. The development of psychology and concepts of mental illness through history will be reviewed with particular emphasis on changing concepts within society and how these affect our ideas of mental health and happiness.

A comparison of divergent religious groups shows that they have far more in common than their followers might suspect, or in some cases, be willing to admit. When basic and crucial elements of these religions are compared, there are essential elements of common ground that should create a bond of understanding and mutual respect. In particular, the concepts of what constitutes a productive member of a religious community, and what constitutes individual happiness show much in common.

A comparison of major schools of psychology shows that they too have much in common even though their adherents are not particularly fond of admitting that fact. Concepts of mental illness show virtually the same elements in each school. Concepts of causative factors and treatment show far more variability between schools of thought. Each school, even ones claiming absolute science as their starting point, place varying degrees of emphasis on spiritual aspects of mental well-being. In the end, each school admits to something more than a belief in heredity and the random firing of neurons as the basis for human behavior. In the end, each school wants to believe in something beyond the mundane elements of daily life as a basis for mental health and happiness.

Both the major religions we will examine and the major schools of psychology show great similarities in their concepts of what constitutes the "good life." The golden rule appears to actually be a major element in all of these diverse religions and schools of psychology. A good life, a mentally healthy life, has virtually the same elements in common. To be happy, we must act with kindness and generosity towards others; we must see beyond the momentary pleasure of an instant and realize what real happiness means; we must make our lives mean something that makes us greater than the small moments of our fragile lives; we must make our lives mean something and in so doing, become part of a greater good. This thread of service to others, and need for ethical and moral behavior can be found in each of the religions examined and in each of the major schools of psychology. The treatment of mental illness needs more than a simple concept of impaired neuro-transmitters and resolving childhood conflicts. To be truly happy, and to be a productive member of a society and a religion, we must deal with the spiritual needs of the individual. Unless these needs are addressed, all other considerations – wealth, power, fame – are meaningless. Since these elements transcend divergent religions, cultures, and schools of psychology, their importance has a face validity that is difficult to deny.

Make us happy
and
you make us
good.

- Robert Browning,
The Ring and the Book

Chapter 1 - A Happy Life

America, possibly more than any other civilization in history, sells the "happy life" as an inalienable, individual right of its citizens. Everyday Americans are bombarded with ads for material possessions and beauty products that will provide this happy life. For the majority of us, however, acquiring these marvelous products does not produce the joy that the marketer insists must accompany their possession.

Many Americans feel cheated when they wake up with all their acquired wealth, plastic surgery improvements, and fifteen minutes of fame only to realize that they have not managed to buy the one thing they really wanted – true happiness. When we look at other countries and cultures, they appear to be increasingly seeking the American ideal of mass consumption and display of wealth as markers of happiness.

The vast majority of us want to be happy, discounting some particular forms of mental illness, and all of us spend our lives seeking contentment – the long-term reality of happiness. It is important to differentiate between moments of joy and happiness, and a life that is lived in contentment and enjoyment. Each of us experiences moments when we have accomplished some goal or some immediate pleasure, but such moments pass and may appear only as markers in time of the few instances of happiness we have experienced within a landscape otherwise bereft of joy. Each of also questions from time to time the meaning of life and whether our lives makes any difference in the grand scheme of things within the immense universe of time, space and matter that surrounds us. While we may not be scholars of philosophy and religion, the same age old questions come to each of us. What does it all mean and how can we find our own individual happiness within the complex world in which we live?

Our country is in the midst of an epidemic of drug abuse. The Department of Health and Human Resources indicates that in 2002 there where 3,120,000 Americans with serious drug problems needing treatment.[1] Obviously, the major reason to take drugs is to change your state of consciousness, to change it to one that is deemed happier. If so many of us cannot face the world without recourse to drugs and altered states of consciousness, it demonstrates that simple instances of immediate joy do not hold the key to true happiness and contentment. While these illicit drugs certainly produce momentary euphoria they cannot grant what is not theirs to give – long term contentment. There obviously must be other elements that form the basis of true happiness.

The number of very wealthy and famous individuals appearing daily in the newspapers with stories of suicide, attempted suicide, family abuse, acts of violence and indications of despair continue to increase. Apparently just having money and fame do not insure the happiness we all seek no matter what the mass marketing moguls claim.

Plastic surgery is now one of the largest growing healthcare segments in America. We seem to be saying that if you look pretty, you will be happy; a nice looking nose and a full head of hair are stepping-stones to happiness. Yet, newspapers and magazines are also full of stories of the young and beautiful, and their seemingly never-ending heartbreaks. Beauty, wealth, power, and fame in themselves do not appear to be the panacea for sadness that advertising agencies would have us believe.

Possibly no statistics reveal the dilemma more vividly than the fact our national suicide rate grows each year. More people die from suicide in America then from homicide at a rate almost two to one. The richest country in the world has an increasing suicide rate. In 2000 there were 29,350 suicides. Suicide is the eleventh leading cause of death for the general population and the third leading cause of death for individuals fifteen to twenty-five years of age.[2] It seems almost unbelievable that suicide would be the third leading cause of death in youthful Americans. How can we have so much and still have so little that suicide is viewed as the only way out for so many adolescents and youth? It is of vital importance that we understand the real elements that form the basic building blocks of contentment and a well-lived life. Before we can help someone attain them, we must be able to identify them.

How can a therapist or counselor help someone attain happiness if he or she does not really know the variables that make up happiness? How can we honestly say that we are making our best effort to guide someone through a therapeutic process if we do not really understand the goals of the process?

The present work examines three major religions and three major schools of psychology in relation to their concepts of being a productive member of the religion and a mentally healthy, happy individual. In this way important variables common to all may be identified. If even divergent belief systems place importance on the same variables, their real importance in contributing to the stated goals are better validated. With common elements noted across diverse religions, cultures and schools of psychology we have correlated variables accepted by the diverse populations that may be used as a guide to establish meaningful guidelines for the therapeutic process.

Chapter 2 - Religion and Psychology

This work will examine three major religions and three major schools of psychology to see if there are any variables common to all which identify a moral and happy life. The major written works within the religions and commentaries on the religions will be reviewed. The diverse sects and minor differences of opinions within the religions will not be discussed unless they point to a controversy affecting the variables we are analyzing. Minor points of divergence within schools of psychology will also not be addressed unless they deal with conflicts specific to our topic.

The three religions chosen for analysis have vastly differing concepts concerning God. They were chosen, however, because they represent an immense number of different ethnic groups and appear in virtually every country on the face of the earth. There are approximately one billion, nine hundred thousand Christians, nine hundred million Hindus, and three hundred million Buddhists. This work will give far more background to Hinduism and Buddhism than Christianity. This is done because the author presumes the reader will have more knowledge of Christianity than the other religions and consequent to this, the reader needs to be presented with information that will allow a better understanding of the development of Hinduism and Buddhism.

Elements of each religion dealing with a prescription for a moral and happy life will be identified. Variables common to all three religions denoting a moral and happy life will be noted. These elements will be considered as having highly significant levels of validity since they have been held in common over great amounts of time, and between very diverse population groups.

The three schools of psychology were chosen because they represent divergent points of view within the profession, and the majority of professionals identify their practice with one of these three schools of thought. The concepts of the three schools in relation to what constitutes a healthy and happy life will be examined. Those elements common to all three schools will be identified. Again, elements held in common by all three schools of psychology will be considered to have the most significant levels of validity.

Religion, philosophy and psychology, obviously have much in common in that each searches for answers to the same age-old questions – what is the meaning of life, what is reality, what is truth and what is happiness. While psychologists state that all of their work is based on science and religious leaders rely on faith for some concepts within their belief system, both search for answers to very similar questions. If we can identify variables that both accept as of paramount importance in finding happiness and contentment, we have established a common base of concepts that all agree upon. Variables concerning the moral and happy life which appear in all three religions and all three schools of psychology will be identified. These variables have a different form of validity. Not only are they correlated within an arena of divergent religions, or schools of psychology, they are correlated between religious beliefs and the science of psychology. These elements give us the best basis for designing treatment and counseling programs because they have stood the test of time and scientific analysis and have validity in different ethnic groups, cultures and religions.

Chapter 3 - Hinduism

Hinduism is difficult to understand even for those within the religious community because it is more a system of religious beliefs than a statement of a specific concept of a single deity. While there are groups within Hinduism that identify a single all-powerful deity, they hold other deities as simply manifestations, avatars, of the one great deity. The beginnings of the Hindu belief system are generally accepted as having occurred with the Aryan invasion around 1500 B.C.[3]

It is important to note that the invasion took place over hundreds of years and it is difficult to know which beliefs were brought by the invaders and which were assimilated by the Aryans into their belief system. To this day scholars have been unable to discern the homeland from which the invaders migrated in their invasion of India. Researchers have placed their point of origin from the Caucasus to the Hungarian plains. The Aryans conquered the Dravidians who where an agricultural and settled people inhabiting the area we now call India. There had been other invasions from the North as some of the sacred texts of Hinduism contain meteorological and astronomical data that places their point of origin in the uplands of Northern Asia. Unlike the Aryans, however, these invaders did not stay, but left their indelible mark within the early religious texts.[4]

These ancient texts are collectively referred to as the *Vedas*. These works contain details on agriculture, appropriate sacrifices to various deities, and proscriptions for behavior, worship and human interaction. As time has gone by many of the material in these texts have been reinterpreted as parables or symbolic representations. The development of a concept of a single divine entity progresses through the *Vedas*. Early writings are concerned with the *devas* and the *asuras*. These represent opposing forces of good and evil, light and darkness, within the world.[5]

These early writings place no emphasis on one group being more powerful or more worthy than the other. They are seen as the reality of the world – a balance of two opposing systems. Over time the importance of given deities changes significantly. Dyaus Pitar is the sky father in early texts, but becomes of virtually no importance in later works. In the middle period of these writing Indra, the king of gods, Ushas, the dawn, and Varuna, who controls the waters of the world, take center stage. Next Angel, the fire god, and Soma, the spirit of intoxication, become paramount in the *Vedas*. In later writings Siva, Brahma and Vishnu have displaced the early deities and become the prime movers within the world of men. As the culmination of this process, Brahma encompasses all aspects of divinity within his single being.

Vishnu is the governing lord of the material world that can be understood by men. He is the fabric of the universe that can be known by the senses. The avatars of Vishnu are numerous and Hindus have been able to incorporate virtually every aspect of other religions, including Buddha and Christ, into avatars of Vishnu.

The *Vedas* indicate that Vishnu controls all that is in heaven and earth. He obtained his dominion of these regions by disguising himself as a dwarf and entertaining other devas at a banquet. He provided such wonderful entertainment that the other devas granted him one request of his choosing. He asked for possession of as much space as he could cover in three steps. The other devas readily granted his request as they presumed that a dwarf could find little reward in such an endeavor. Vishnu then changed his form and proceeded to step across the heavens and the earth. He did not take so large a step that would have granted him the underworlds, for Hindus believe it is unwise to claim too much.[6] Vishnu is one of the most revered devas in Hinduism as he represents all that is good in the material universe. He is seen as a benevolent and cheerful representation of the spirit of the divine that runs like a river of divinity connecting every aspect of the world we can know through the senses.

To better understand the changes in Hinduism that led to
Brahma, Siva and Vishnu becoming the most revered of deities
who are incorporated into the concept of a single all-powerful
deity, the periods of development can be divided into five segments of time:

The Indus Valley Civilization, circa 2500 B.C.-1750 B.C.

A Vedic Age, circa 1200 B.C.-200 B.C.

An Epic Age, circa 400 B.C.-800 A.D.

Medival South Asia, circa 750 A.D.-1750 A.D.

Modern South Asia, circa 1750-the present[7]

While every living religion shows changes over time, Hinduism evolved in an extremely complex manner during these periods. Still the basic concepts of a good and moral life remained
relatively constant.

Civilization in India developed around the Indus River. The
earliest name in Sanskrit for this river was Sindhu. Our designation of Hindu actually comes from the name of the river.

The land in this area is extremely fertile because it is in a
flood plain. The early inhabitants were farmers and excavations
at Mohenjo-daro, Harrapa, and Kalibangan reveal an extremely
complex and well organized civilization. While we have a great
deal of information from archeological evidence of this
civilization's economic and social order, there is little concerning their religious beliefs or practices. There are numerous archeological findings indicating religious practices and ritual buri-
als, but there is no written evidence to reveal the nature of any
formalized religion. The actual contribution of these early cul-

tures to the religious beliefs of Hinduism may be understood after further archeological excavations presently in progress throughout Northern India are completed.

The earliest religious texts appear during the Vedic period. The four early collections of verses are known as the *Samhitas* – the *Rigveda*, *Yajurveda*, *Samaveda*, and the *Atharvaveda*. Indra, a war god with an invincible thunderbolt, appears most frequently in theses texts. His major advisory is Vritra, an evil cloud serpent who spends his time withholding water and light from mankind.

Varuna is a sky god and the guardian of a cosmic order. Mitra is another sky god who appears as a kind of mediator between the other gods. Agni is the fire god and in some ways is the energy source within all things. Soma is the god of intoxication; the inspiration of poets and priests, and the source of insight, strength and immortality. The Ashvin twins are pastoral deities connected with the fertility of herds, crops and humans.

Rudra is god both of destruction and creation. He is mercurial and can change aspects from good to evil in an instant. His sons are the Maruts, or Rudras, who are minor deities. One of Rudra's aspects is Shiva, "auspicious," and as such, Shiva becomes of great importance in later literature and Hindu thought.[8]

Surya is a sun god who warms the earth. Yama is the lord of the dead. Asditi is a mother goddess. Saravasti is a river goddess providing nurture for crops. There are numerous other gods appearing in the Vedas. The ones mentioned are those that appear most frequently in the texts.

There are three basic world view concepts found in these early Vedic writings, and they form the foundation of Hindu thought. The first of these beliefs is that the universe is the product of the sacrificed body (yajina) of a great cosmic being. Second, mankind has a responsibility to refabricate and sacrifice anew this cosmic entity. Mankind regenerates the world through spiritual knowledge and effort, or karma. Third there exists in the world two great forces: fire and plant. These forces must be activated by man through ritualistic and spiritually appropriate actions. If this is not done, the world will cease.

Understanding these basic concepts helps us to understand why there was, and to a lesser extent still is, so much ritual in the daily lives of Hindus. The Vedas contain directions on how to perform appropriately virtually every aspect of life, including guidelines for the individual and society. According to the Vedas, unless all these rituals are performed, the universe ceases.

Contained within the rituals was the concept of eternal life, we live on in some form after each cycle of death. The rituals in the Vedas enabled the individual to ensure his or her transcendence beyond the present life form. That is why the instructions in the Vedas take up so many of the sutras; they are essential to the concept of immortality.

This order in all things also manifested itself in the cast system. In the Vedic period there are three major casts, each of which has specific functions tied to the world order. Brahmanas were priests who taught and monitored the expression of prayer and sacrifice, and guided others towards the correct path through life. Rajanyas, or Kshatriyas, were the warrior class who guarded the populace against all invaders and demons. Vaishyas were the class of commerce and work. Later, another caste, Shudra, was added at the lowest end of the cast system. This was prob ably a designation for subjugated people that later applied to anyone seen as being in the lowest rung of the social ladder. Even later during this period certain forms of work deemed beneath human dignity, such as touching defiled materials, established a different caste, the untouchables. This last cast during this period was deemed to be outside of the margins of human society.[9]

From these initial caste systems, an intricate social order arose. People were not allowed to marry outside their caste. Different laws governed the interaction within these communities.

In the Epic Period, attention turned from the ritualistic elements of the Vedas to the *Upanishads*, or learned discussions and debates. During this period some of the most crucial concepts in Hindu religion were analyzed in great depth. Central to all of these issues is death.

The ideas of *samsara*, the wheel of life and death, is not found in the early Vedas, making it extremely unlikely that it was of Aryan origin. This concepts appears only later in the Upansihads. Transmigration of the soul is not an idea that appears frequently in Western thought before this period. Even Pythagoras was affected by Oriental thought in the development of his transmigration theory.[10]

Initially the wheel of life appears to be an incredible gift to mankind. We never die; we just appear in another format. Just as Vinshu never dies and has avatars that die for him, humans never die; they simply enter the wheel of life in some new manifestation.

Is this not the immortality that all of us so desperately seek? It is immortality, but it is also endless death and suffering. All of

the misery that each of us experience will never end, it goes on
through all time. Also, only our deeds in each life will determine
how we are to be reborn. We can come back as any number of
not very palatable possibilities. One can come back as a blade
of grass, a goat, a vulture, a snake, a pig or any number of alter-
natives that do not lend themselves to happy living.

Man is like the Flying Dutchman, or the Wandering Jew,
doomed to live forever between heaven and hell. The slightest
mistake can lead us back to life as a wild animal or a domestic
pet. No act is random or accidental as far as Hindu thought is
concerned. Everything happens for a reason, and that reason is
the individual. Whatever happens, happens due to the individual.
No matter how accidental an event may appear; it occurs due to
the actions or thoughts of the individual, or the individuals affected by the event. No religion places any higher level of responsibility for what happens to a person in life than Hinduism.

A tree that falls in the woods upon the woodcutter fell due
to the actions or thoughts of the woodcutter. For the Hindu of
this time such an event would be no different than shooting an
arrow at a target and hitting the target. He who shot the arrow
is responsible for what is struck. The tiniest error in judgment
or behavior can lead to awesome consequences, and these consequences can effect many trips on the wheel of samsara. This
concept is in many ways extremely frightening. The idea of
being doomed for thousands of years due to a single bad behavior is a punishment that does not seem to fit the crime. This
concept, however, is central to Hindu thought.

In this religion your past is your accumulated future. Every
action, every thought is held forever within this wheel of life

and death. As your past falls behind you, it constructs your future by adding and subtracting acts that are good and evil until they play out in the next life, thus constructing your next future life.

Nothing within the wheel of samsara depends on any deity. There are no mitigating circumstances, no one who can help you to overcome even the smallest errors in judgment. There are few religions were man is so alone with his own evil deeds. There are no forces that help, for samsara is a phenomenon like gravity. It is just a never-ending reality.

Our karma decides our future, our present and our past. During the Epic Period, karma has come to mean both our spiritual knowledge and effort, and the sum of each and every action weighed in relation to good and evil. The accounting system is absolutely perfect. All our behavior is measured within the meaning of karma. It is the essence of "What goes around, comes around." The smallest mistake is paid back in exact measure. There is no appeals system and there is no one who can accept your burden for you. No sin can be forgiven and no good deed will go without payment. For each action there is a perfect accord between its weight of good and evil, and the return that you will inevitably receive. This does not mean that it will be immediate or that you will recognize it when it appears. It means the balance of actions with rewards or punishment is fixed and must occur either in this life, or in the calculation of what you will be in the next life you must face.

There is no word for "chance" in Sanskrit or early Indian languages.[11] It is difficult for the Western mind to comprehend the idea that there simply is no belief in chance during this period of Hindu thought. However, when you realize that the language had no word for such a concept, it would be hard to believe that those who spoke the language believed in such a possibility.

Since nothing falls by chance upon us, the wheel of samsara is absolutely just. Those who perform ritual and spiritual acts, and perform good deeds can have future incarnations as humans. Those who do not perform ritual and spiritual acts, and do not perform good deeds take lower and lower paths on the wheel of life and death.

There is a way out of this endless cycle of death and rebirth. Those who achieve true knowledge of the "path of the gods" can be released from the cycle. These individuals have achieved *moksha* and are free of samsara.[12] Note that the religious emphasis has changed from relatively mindless ritual acts to contemplation of self and the world within which you exist. No longer can you achieve release by ritual acts governing virtually every aspect of life. While these must be present, their importance has been relegated to a secondary level.

Only through introspection and a mystical union with the atmanbrahaman, the being of being, can one achieve true happiness and release.[13] This is the beginning of Hindu mystical thought concerning intricate forms of meditation. In order to rid ourselves of the elements that hold us to the wheel of life and death, we must understand what is meaningful and what is not meaningful; we must understand the essence of self and its relation to the being of being. While each of our deeds is still written in the book of karma, in order to free ourselves of the wheel we must understand the "why" of the writing. Individual thought has become more important than individual ritual acts.

The next steps in the evolution of Hinduism occur during the Medieval South Asia Period. A subtle change has already happened with differing concepts of good and evil. Previously good and evil have simply been two sides of a single coin with neither being of more importance, or being more powerful that its opposite. The Ramayana texts begin to place good in a different position and suggest that good will triumph. Hindu ideas concerning good and evil become much more like Western tradition. In previous texts, the characters representing evil have attributes that certainly could be considered admirable – there are more areas of gray in relation to what constitutes good and what constitutes evil. In later works, there is a clear distinction between the aspects of good and evil.[14]

It is important to note that during this period Hinduism comes in direct contact with Islam. There were invasions beginning in the seventh century. By 1600 Akbar, the Mughal emperor, ruled virtually all of what is now India, Pakistan and Bangledesh.

Possibly this contact and subjugation led Hindu scholars and priests to explore the depths of their religion with a renewed intensity. Two great Brahman scholars, Shankara and Ramanuja appear during this era.

Shankara posited that there is only one true reality – Brahman, the true Self. Shankara's interpretation of past texts is that only Brahman exists without duality; consequently only *brahman* is real. Brahman, the true Self, is not held within the wheel of samsara because *brahman* does not suffer from ignorance, *avidya,* and illusions, *maya.* For an individual to reach enlightenment and rid himself of the wheel of life and death, he must rid himself of wrong knowledge, *avidya,* and obtain knowledge of the brahman.[15]

Shankara has reinterpreted the previous texts in the Upanishads and the Vedas to produce a theistic concept. He is stating that the text is allegorical and symbolic; it is not an explanation of the truth, but a puzzle leading the true believer to a truth not immediately revealed. The many stories concerning good and evil are simply ways of conveying truths to mankind in a format that they can understand and identify with and were never meant to be truths in and of themselves. Just as a parable attempts to reveal a truth by leading us through an interesting story to a meaningful end product, a truth about reality or an indication of the essence of a good life, the previous Hindu texts have been only a vehicle to carry us toward the truth we seek.

The gods mentioned in the texts are simply manifestations of a single being. They present different aspects of a single reality. According to Shankara they should be seen as explaining complex truths in a simplistic form necessary to lead the reader toward true knowledge.

Shankara saw the single all encompassing deity as impersonal and without qualities, while being all qualities. The next great teacher of this period, Ramanuja, saw the one deity as being quite different in nature from Shankara's concept.

Ramanuja was a teacher in the Tamil Nadu probably during the early twelfth century. He wrote extensive commentaries on the Upanishads, the *Brahma Sutras* and the *Bhagavad Gita.*

Ramanuja's concepts of the single deity were greatly influenced by the Tamil Alvars. The Alvars were poets who wrote the attributes of god and his works within the world of men. One of the most famous Alvars, and the one most affecting Ramanuja's writings was Nammalvar. His one god is extremely personal and has all the attributes of splendor and divine beauty that are absent in Shankara's writings.[16]

Shankara maintained that the knowledge of rituals was meaningless in relation to the knowledge of the Self, the one truth. Only knowledge of the Self is important. Ramanuja states that truth comes from all kinds of knowledge and is not limited to simply finding the singularity of the brahman. Ramanuja held that there was a oneness of knowledge that flowed equally through all these possibilities.

In Shankara's writings the individual self is only an illusion that causes nothing but misery. The way out of samsara is to return, through knowledge, to the one true Self. By returning to the Self and giving up the painful illusion of individuality, we break the chains that bind us to the never-ending cycle of life and death. All sadness and despair are caused by this illusion; and the evil acts that we commit are caused by ignorance of these truths leading to our return to samsara.

Ramanuja's theology states the existence of the individual self. The self is eternal and cannot be destroyed. The bad deeds that we commit in life and our failure to see into the reality of the one true God can bind us in the wheel of life and death, but we are forever individuals with our destiny.

Ramanuja's concepts of theism became the mainstream of thought for Hindu religion. His concepts of a single deity with many representations and his concepts of the eternal and individual nature of the human continue in Hindu tradition even now.

After Ramanuja's death, two major sects with differing interpretations of his teaching emerged. The dividing element is the nature of how an individual can be saved. Both sects agree that knowledge of the Self and righteous behaviors lead to salvation, or breaking the wheel of samsara. The question revolves around the mechanism of salvation.

The story of the differences between the sects is told by way of the actions of two animal mothers. When a kitten is in danger, the mother cat picks up the kitten by the neck and takes the kitten to safety. A baby monkey, when faced with danger, jumps on its mother's back and holds on until safety is reached. In the first instance, only the mother's actions are of true importance. In the second instance, it is the behavior of the baby monkey that is paramount in its salvation.

While good deeds are important to both sects, one sect denies that human initiative is of prime importance in release from samsara. For this sect, only divine grace can pull man from the wheel of life and death into true knowledge and happiness. Man must give himself up completely to the deity in order for salvation to occur. With this absolute surrender to the deity, the individual no longer commits sinful acts because his nature becomes part of the deity and salvation is assured. The other sect maintains that divine grace is needed, but human initiative is the critical element in finding salvation. While both sects emphasize the absolute importance of good deeds, one sect states that only the given grace of oneness in the deity allows salvation.[17] It is interesting to note that elements of these same arguments appear in Christianity, Buddhism and Islam.

By the time of the Modern South Asia period, the power of the Mughals had been broken and new invaders had appeared. By the late 1700's the British Empire had established itself as the dominant force in India. England maintained this empire until India achieved independence on January 26, 1947.

A number of extremely influential teachers appeared within the Hindu tradition during this period. Ram Mohan Roy, a Bengali Brahman, was greatly influenced by the new dominant power and studied in England. He became familiar with Christianity and Islam. The intricate network of sacrifices and rituals, and the extremely convoluted assemblages of gods or representations of gods, came to be seen by Ram Mohan Ray as superfluous to the true Hindu religion. He saw the *Upanishads* as explaining the existence of the one true God.

Another teacher during this period, and one known far better in American culture, is Ramakrishna. He was also a Bengali Brahman and a temple priest. His beliefs traveled far from his humble beginnings. Ramakrishna was a mystic who combined elements of numerous religions and religious traditions. Yoga, Tantrism, Vedanta, Vashinava theism, Christianity, and Islam. The most important element for Ramakrishna was the feminine power worshiped as the goddess Kali. This was a theistic belief, as only the concept of an unending kindness is represented in Kali, even when Kali appears other than gentle or giving. Central to Ramakrishna's belief is the necessity of providing charity and kindness to all our fellow beings. The Ramakrishna movement was brought to many other countries through the influence of Vivekanaga, a follower of Ramakrishna .

Aurobindo was another well-known teacher during this period. He was also influenced by Western traditions and education. His most important work was *The Last Divine*. This work tells in both logical dialectic and allegories how man can progress from primal matter to perfection within the Self where all is bliss and happiness. There is now an international center for spiritual transformation based on his teaching in Poindecherry, South India.[18]

There is another great teacher from this period whose name is instantly known around the world, Mohanda Karamchand Gandhi, the Mahatma or "Great Soul." He was also influenced by a western education along with his readings in Hindu traditional texts. He saw the horrors of human conflict firsthand in the Boer War where he served as a medical attendant with the Bristish Army. The first concentration camps were actually created by the British in order to subjugate the Boers who where helped by the local population. By concentrating Boer civilians in these horrible camps, the British were able to isolate the Boears from supplies and other civilian aid. Gandhi came home a different man from the youth who had gone to war for the British. He was horrified by these startling demonstrations of man's inhumanity to his fellow beings. This was the birth of his program of nonviolence, *ahimsa*. During the rest of his life, Gandhi fought against the caste system and all forms of violence that could be inflicted on other begins. He was killed by a Hindu extremist and was unable to prevent the violence that has so plagued relations between Hindus and Muslims.

Over these periods of transition there have been many changes in Hindu beliefs and it remains an extraordinarily complex religion to outsiders. While Hinduism was not a religion spread by conquest, during the past two centuries it has formed religious communities in numerous countries including America, Canada, many countries in South America and Indonesia. Each of these communities have established different interpretations of ideas within Hindu tradition. There are elements that can be identified, however, as basic to the religion. These are core concepts of the religion that transcend different sects and geographical locations. It is these fundamental principles that define the very nature of the religion itself and affect the daily lives of those who practice Hinduism. The following are core concepts concerning leading a good and happy life:

Each of us is responsible for our actions.

What we do unto others will be done to us.

We are not allowed to kill our fellow beings or act in such a way as to allow this to occur.

We are not allowed to steal from others or to countenance those who steal from others

If we incite or direct others in evil acts we are equally responsible for their behavior.

Charity to others is a requirement for leading a good life.

We must show respect for age and wisdom.

We must be kind and generous to our fellow beings.

A meaningful life involves services to our fellow beings.

To reach a union with God we must purge our minds of greed, envy and all wrongful desires and actions.

When these core elements are examined, they obviously have far more in common with Christianity than might be expected after our trip through the maze of Vedas, Upanishads, and the Ramayana. After the elements of the religion which are specific to its culture heritage are removed, the similarities to Christian directives for leading a good and happy life are amazingly similar. Now let us turn to an exploration of the roots of Buddhism and its core beliefs.

Chapter 4 - Buddhism

The founder of Buddhism, Gautama Siddhartha, was born in 560 B.C. His family was relatively wealthy and lived in northern India in the foothills of the Himalayas. Little is known about his early years except that they were spent in relative luxury. He married when he was sixteen or nineteen, there are differing accounts among scholars, but all agree that his wife was a paragon of wifely virtues.[19] While in his late twenties Gautama, along wih his wife and family, took up life as a simple Brahmin mendicant.

His abrupt departure from this life of luxury is explained by later disciples as an epiphany brought on by witnessing the sad-

ness of life for the first time. It is said that his father had shel-
tered him from all forms of sadness, and that before his period
of initial enlightenment he had never seen the infirmities of
age, sickness or physical deformity, or death. Upon seeing these
parts of life, Gautama was stricken with the horrors that life
could bring, and devoted himself to trying to understand and
overcome them.

Gautama devoted himself to Brahmin philosophy and became the disciple of Alara Kalama. With Kalama he studied
how to obtain the "realm of nothingness" through prolonged
periods of meditation. Gautama was dissatisfied with these tech-
niques and found that he could not obtain the enlightment he
sought, He left his teacher and found another famous Brahmin
philosopher Uddaka Ramaputta, with whom he studied.

Again, Gautama was unable to find the enlightenment he
sought. He decided to seek enlightenment by testing the concepts of extreme asceticism advocated by Jainism. For five years
Gaqutama practiced these tenants of extreme asceticism. His
body became incredibly emaciated and it is said that on some
days he lived on a single fruit for the whole day.[20]

At the end of these five years, Gautama found himself so
weak that he could barely move, but found himself no closer to
enlightenment. He had tried both of the paths that the major
religions had directed, meditation and self-mortification, and still
he could not find what he sought.[21]

Gautama then set himself under the Bodhi tree, determined
to stay until he had found the knowledge that would free him
from the sadness of the world around him. He found the answer he sought. Wrong desire, rising out of the primal will to

live and have, was the cause of all sadness. He then passed into a state of ecstasy culminating in poised equanimity and mindfulness.[22] Gautama was convinced that for him, "Rebirth is no more; I have lived the highest life; my task is done, and now for me there is no more of what I have been."[23] He had found the enlightenment he sought and experienced an adumbration of Nirvana. He became the Buddha, the Enlightened One.

This is when Buddha made the decision to stay in the world of men so that he could become a teacher for others and show them the path to wisdom and contentment. He was tempted to remain in Nirvana and not be burdened with the struggle of teaching others what he had learned, but he overcame this temptation and sought out disciples that he might enlighten others.

He began with five disciples as advocates for his concept of the "middle way." Neither lust nor self-mortification could find the truth. The middle way is between two extremes, and advocates insight leading to wisdom, which leads to contentment and on to knowledge and enlightenment. This was the beginning of the *Sangha*, the Buddhist monastic order.[24] Buddha wandered through Northern India and his disciples rose to sixty.

The order began to adopt rules for the disciples. They wore yellow robes, had shaved heads, carried a begging bowl and practiced daily meditation. All disciples also had to obey the Ten Precepts:

Refrain from destroying life.
Do not take what is not given.
Abstain from unchastity.
Do not lie or deceive.

Abstain from intoxicants.

Eat moderately and not after noon.

Do not look on dancing, singing, or dramatic spectacles.

Do not effect the use of garland, scent, unguents or
ornaments

Do no use high or broad beds.

Do not accept gold or silver.[25]

It is interesting to note that the Buddha recognized that some disciples could reach all the intended goals of the Ten Precepts and that others, though well meaning, could not. He set up a lay-associates order. These individuals vowed to uphold the Five Precepts, the first five of the indicated Ten Precepts.

Over his years of teaching the Buddha developed a great following of disciples. Many of the first disciples were from his own family. The Buddha's cousin Ananada is one of his most famous disciples. During this period of development many women also sought to be disciples. At first the Buddha refused, but later relented and admitted women to the teaching order.

He is reported to have said, "Ananada, if women had not received permission to enter the Order, the pure religion would have lasted a thousand years, but since they have received permission, it will stand fast for only five hundred years".[26] At least in this one concept the Buddha appears to have erred as the Order has lasted over twenty-five hundred years.

The Buddha's decision to admit lay disciples and nuns was extremely effective in spreading the Order throughout India. It was this core of lay disciples who gave the land and wealth necessary to create monasteries to provide centers of Buddhist teaching throughout the country. His repudiation of the caste system also led to the acceptance of his teachings among the vast number of lower casts in India. The Buddha's own connection to higher castes insured that money and land would be available.

The Buddha himself passed away after 45 years of teaching near the town of Kuisnara, northeast of Benares. He was eighty years of age and had founded a religion that would endure, but would change greatly over time. It is important to remember that the Buddha began his learning process following Hindu priests. We have seen the complex and intricate formulation of Hindu texts and their emphasis on speculative and esoteric philosophy. Possibly part of the Buddha's teaching was a reaction to the ritualism and mysticism of his Hindu teachers. The Buddha emphasized practical applications of logic and reason to the most vital questions facing mankind. He was in many ways more interested in the psychology of the mind and religion than in metaphysics. He repudiated the convoluted speculations of Hindu tradition within which he had been raised:

"Bear always in mind what it is I have not elucidated, and what it is that I have elucidated. And what I have not elucidated? I have not elucidated that the world is eternal; I have not elucidated that the world is finite; I have not elucidated that the soul and body are identical; I have not elucidated that the monk who has attained arahat exists after death; I have not elucidated that the arahat exists after death; I have not elucidated that the arahat nether exists nor does not exist after death. And why have I not elucidated this? Because this profits not, nor has to do with the fundamentals of religion; therefore I have not elucidated this."[27]

There is obviously a great deal that the Buddha has not elucidated. Each of the non-elucidation statements refers to areas of philosophical speculation that are very important in Hindu texts. The Buddha is deliberately distancing himself and his concepts from the Vedic tradition and later commentaries. He is stating that his religion concentrates on thoughts and actions that have direct importance in the lives of his followers:

"And what have I elucidated? Misery I have elucidated; the origin of misery I have elucidated; the cessation of misery I have elucidated; and the path leading to the prophet has to do with fundamentals of religion, and tends to an absence of passion, to knowledge, supreme wisdom and Nirvana."[28]

Buddha is stating that it is not man's philosophy or speculations on concepts that man cannot understand, but man's feelings that are of paramount importance in salvation. We must understand the nature of evil desires and extirpate them from our being in order to reach Nirvana.

During this period of Buddhist development it is important to note that the Buddha did not believe in a supreme being who was eternal and immune to the cycle of death and rebirth. He did believe in gods and goddesses and in forces beyond human understanding, but he held all of these to be subject to the Hindu concept of transmigration of the soul. He held the Hindu concepts of karma and samsara to be a reality, but he changed the meaning of each. The concept of karma becomes more lenient and less absolute in relation to the consequences of any single, minute act.

If we give up evil desires and follow the path of kindness to all life, we will end our cycle within samsara. This does not mean, however, that we achieve eternal bliss as the singular entity we believe ourselves to be, for this supposed singularity is part of another allusion. Buddha states that what we consider an immortal soul actually consists of a momentary amalgamation of ever changing states of being, *skandhas*.

There are five of these states: the body, sensations, feelings, *sankharas* (a kind of collective unconscious married with instincts) and reason.[29] What we see as an individual human is actually a fleeting aggregation of these five elements of existence. Each of these elements is in constant flux much like the electrons, positrons, neutrons and other subatomic particles within an electrical motor. Superficially these appear constant. When we die these elements break apart. Only these sankharas fall into an eternal reality. The singularity of an individual lasts only a split second in time, but the subatomic particles of which it is composed continue their existence and may come again one day to form another electrical motor or a blade of grass. This is one of the most disturbing elements of the Buddha's teachings and has caused many great debates and schisms within the religion.

Buddha stated that transmigration of the soul does not involve the transmigration of any actual substance. When a machine that stamps out ashtrays falls on a circular disk of cooper, a new ashtray is formed. The machine is the not the ashtray and the formatted stamp is not the ashtray; yet the machine has pasted on in time the imprint of a possibility. The circular plate of cooper would have remained only a circular plate of copper without the action of the stamping machine. The stamp does not itself pass into the next life form; it creates the format for that life form.

An analogy frequently used in late Buddhist commentaries involves the lighting of one candle from another candle. Just as the second candle cannot be lit without the first candle, so can the next transmigration of the soul not occur without the imprint of the previous existence. The first candle does not become the second candle, but it is the reason behind its existence.

This becomes more complex since the Buddha also states that the newborn entity is not different from the former entity, nor is it the same. He is stating that these are not issues since all is illusion save for the reality of the one Being. This one Being is not a sentient god, but the never-ending reality of the oneness of all that exists. Yet beyond all of these statements and in seeming contradiction, the Buddha clearly states that what a man is today will be carried on and on forever even through all time if he does not rid himself of false knowledge and find the true path. The Buddha appears to have meant that these are all meaningless illusions, the reality of which cannot be known until Nirvana is achieved.

As can be seen by these extremely recondite concepts and the Buddha's denial of a sentient god, Buddhism was originally more a philosophy than a religion. When the Buddha's teaching spread to the masses, however, a number of major changes occurred. Due to the fact that Buddha had led an exemplary life with great emphasis on good deeds and kindness to all living beings; it was easy for a cult of worship to develop around his personality. Like Hinduism, so many different sects were to develop that Buddhism became more a collection of religions with critical core elements than a single standardized religion. These differing sects usually centered around a charismatic teacher or group of teachers.

After the death of Buddha, tradition has it that five hundred of the Buddha's disciples gathered to recite all the sayings and teachings of Buddha. Present day scholars believe that it was actually another two hundred years before these teachings were put in writing in the *Tripitaka*, *Three Baskets*. The "Vinaya Pitaka" details monastic rules. The "Sutta Pitaka" is a series of discourses said to come directly from the teachings of Buddha. The "Abhidama Pitaka" is a series of interpretations of the teachings of the Buddha and their implications in daily life. This last is of great importance because it details how to live a moral and happy life in order to reach salvation.[30] While Buddha's disciples did much to make Buddhism a popular religion, the greatest impetus in expanding Buddhist's teachings came from Asoka, one of the greatest of the emperors of India. He was the grandson of the famous Chandrgupta who destroyed the Macedonian garrisons left behind by Alexander the Great, and united the majority of what is now India under his rule. Asoka expanded the empire and in so doing caused a great loss of life and much suffering among the subjugated people that apparently affected him greatly. Asoka publicly embraced Buddhism and vigorously attempted to make it the state religion.

Amazingly, Asoka publicly apologized for the deaths and suffering he had caused. He stated that he would forever practice gentleness and kindness to his fellow beings. He stopped the royal hunts that killed hundreds of animals. He forbade the killing of any animal for sport and limited the types of animals that could be used for food.

In a world were ten thousand soldiers could die in a single battle and thousands of animals were slaughtered for sport in royal hunts, this is a truly unusual pronouncement from an all-powerful emperor. It is difficult today to realize what an extraordinary action this was by an emperor who ruled with absolute power. A single word from the emperor could bring about the deaths of thousands, and yet he publicly repudiated his own behavior. He actually stated he had been wrong. One has only to consider modern times and the likelihood of even our relatively powerless leaders publicly stating that they had made even a minor mistake, let alone one that had led to the deaths and suffering of thousands.

Around the country Asoka had Buddhist precepts carved into rocks so that all people could know the right path and the rules that guided this path:

"Thus saith His Sacred Majesty: Father and mother must be hearkened to, similarly respect for living creatures must be firmly established; truth must be spoken. These are the virtues of the Law which must be practiced. Similarly, the teacher must be reverenced by the pupil, and fitting courtesy must be shown to relations. Slaves and servants must be treated properly, teachers must be honored, and there must be gentleness towards all living things and liberality for ascetics and Brahmins."

In all of these pronouncements there is no real reference to the Five Precepts or the Four Nobel Truths. Asoka was trying to provide a series of rules of life which could be easily understood by the common man, and hopefully lead to inclusion in the paradise hereafter.

He drastically changed the very nature of the religion by indicating that anyone can reach a paradise beyond the wheel of life if they will store up merit by their good deeds in the present life. After forty years of rule, Asoka retired to a monastic life.

In many ways, Asoka is more the founder of the religion of Buddhism than Buddha. He raised Buddha to a kind of deity, brought forth the concept of a paradise that can be reached through good deeds, developed simple rules for a moral life, and sent forth missionaries to other countries to spread the religion.

While missionaries worked in Ceylon, Egypt, and Syria, another great leader who would change Buddhism appeared in India around the first century A.D. His name was Kanishka and he ruled in what is now Afghanistan and northwestern India. His capital was in the present-day Peshawar. It is from this period that the curly-headed Buddha images appear which now dominate all Buddhist art forms. This was due to the presence of Greco-Bactrians within the subjugated people ruled by Kanishka who admired their sculpture and put them to the task of creating new images for religion.

Kanishka not only changed the image of the religion, he changed the basic elements of the religion. Guautama Buddha becomes a divine being who came to earth in order to help man extirpate himself from the miseries of life. Gautama had lived many other perfect lives and as such had been during these other lives, a Bodhisattva or future Buddha. There have been many Buddhas, some come to earth to help and others remain in Nirvana. Now there are numerous Buddhas to whom one can pray for guidance and help. No longer is man alone with only his behavior to reach salvation; he can turn to other compassionate beings for both guidance and aid in the struggles of life. These are profound changes that made the religion far more acceptable to far more people. It was a religion for the masses and not for a learned few. Many of the deities of Hinduism were wrapped in the form of Buddhist concepts, allowing an easy transition from Hinduism to Buddhism for a worshiper. All Buddhists did not, however, go along with these changes in the basic elements of their faith. The Hinayanists did not accept the many variations of Bodhisattvas and the concept of divine intervention in human life, although they did believe in the idea that there where many previous Buddhas, and that there would be at least one future Buddha. The Mahayanists promulgated numerous deities and the reality of divine intervention in human life.[32]

The Hinayanists doctrine remained remote to most people and did not travel well beyond the circle of elite intellectuals. Their ideas were complicated and extremely difficult for a layman to understand. The recondite arguments concerning an individual personality existing forever, but not in any formulation that could be understood as a human entity was a little more than most layman wanted to try to understand.

The Mahayanists religion changed as it expanded into new regions and countries. It accepted new Bodhisattvas that mirrored local deities and beliefs. Where Hinayanists had gone and been rejected for their lack of humanistic appeal, Mahayanists prevailed. Mahayanists maintained the morality and ethical demands of the religion, but added elements that could be easily accepted by different cultures. As a result of the willingness of the Mahayanists to absorb local aspects of other religions, they obtained far more converts than the Hinayanists. The Hinayanists form of Buddhism had reached China by at least 65 A.D. We know that the emperor Ming Ti had allowed a statue of Buddha to be erected during this period although Ming Ti did not himself become an adherent to Buddhism.[33]

While some intellectuals apparently embraced the religion, the majority of the Chinese people found the religion both difficult to understand and inimical to both their character and existing religions. The existing religions, or philosophies of Taoism and Confucian, were firmly established and were far less pessimistic about life on the earth than Hinayanists Buddhism.

Around 300 A.D., however, the Mahayanists arrived to a very different welcome. Part of this was due to the fact that China was in a state of turmoil during this period and the world no longer looked quite as appealing as it had under the stability of former emperors. The Mahayanists also incorporated many aspects of existing religions and emphasized those aspects of Buddhism which most appealed to the Chinese culture. The concept of devotion to parents and family was emphasized, and prayers for ancestors were added to Buddhist rites for the dead.

The Mahayanists concept of a paradise in the afterlife also found a receptive audience as existing Chinese religions had no such concepts of a beautiful and eternal place of bliss. The emphasis on individual accomplishments rather than accidents of birth to achieve salvation also found eager acceptance in a culture where the accident of birth could place you forever in servitude.

By the sixth century Buddhism had spread to Korea and become the dominant religion. From Korea emissaries were sent to Kimmei, the emperor of Japan. Legend has it that the emperor allowed an image of Buddha to be placed in an area of the county dominated by the Soga clan to see what effect it might have on the local Kami, native, and regional deities. A pestilence followed and the emperor had the image thrown in a canal. The next emperor tried the same experiment with a new image of the Buddha sent by the Koreans. Again, a pestilence struck the land and the image was thrown into a canal. The pestilence continued, however after the Buddha had established his new watery adobe. The Soga clan decided that it might be the Buddha who was irritated and brought the pestilence.

By the time Suiko became the empress of Japan, Buddhism had become far more widely accepted. By 588 A.D. Shotoku Taishi, an ardent supporter of Buddhism became regent. He totally accepted the humanitarian aspects of Mahayana Buddhism. Shotoku Taishi erected hospitals and alms houses for the poor in the name of the Buddha.[34] Numerous public works were constructed as part of the regent's manifestation of the right of Buddhism.

Needless to say, these many public generosities had a stimulating affect on the acceptance of the religion. While the Japanese national religion of Shinto might have been a formidable stumbling block to general acceptance, the Mahayana Buddhism.simply incorporated all the Kami into the Buddhist pantheon of Buddha's and Bodhistattvas. It was easy to practice both Shinto and Buddhism, as neither were now in conflict.

Mahayana's acceptance of local deities, such as the Kami, placed them in three differing orders: Manushi Buddhas, Bodhisattvas, and Dhyani Buddhas.[36] Manushi Buddhas have reached and remain forever in Nirvana. They have suffered many incarnations and faced the misery of life many times. They have been teachers attempting to guide a man on the right path to salvation. They could have on many occasions simply accepted Nirvana, but they willingly chose to stay on earth to aid man in finding salvation. While they can be prayed to, they do not take part in the lives of men. Their incredible sacrifices for mankind have allowed them to live eternally; undisturbed by any hint of sadness in a never-ending paradise.

In the Hinayana interpretation there are only two Bodhisattvas: Gautama before he accepted Nirvana and Maitreya. In the Mahayana interpretation there is a far larger pantheon of possibilities. Bodhisattvas are beings who have made a vow to become a Buddha. They have lived many exemplary lives and have a virtually inexhaustible store of merit from all the good deeds and acts of compassion they have given to others. They are like ministering angels who watch over mankind. Due to the incredible store of merit they possess, they can give some of this merit to those who pray to them or ask them for guidance. They have abstained from total admittance to Nirvana because they wish to give others part of their merit to make life easier to live and to redirect others to the path of righteous actions.

While Gautama and Maitreya are the most well known of the Boddhisattvas, there are many others who are of greater importance in different countries. In some ways, they have replaced existing local deities. Manjusri and Avalakitesvara (Kwan-Yin in Chinese) are more popular in Southern India and China. Manjusri helps all those who wish to follow the true path by providing guidance and counseling concerning the ways of the Buddha. Avalakitesvara, "The Lord Who Appears to This Age," is the personification of divine compassion. He watches over mankind and protects those devoted to the true path. In China, Avalakitesvara became Kwan-Yin, the goddess of mercy. She is the essence of kindness and generosity and ministers to all of those in need who call on her. It is easy to understand how these figures could draw the support of the multitude and so easily eclipse the Hinhayana concepts.

Dhyani Buddha's concept of "Buddhas of Contemplation" have also not accepted eternal salvation in Nirvana, but they do not achieve their merit by appearing in numerous incarnations as humans. They continually sit in contemplation and actively aid mankind by answering their prayers and directing them towards the true path. Vairoca, Bhaisajyaguru, and Amitabha are the most widely known in Western literature.[36] Amitabha has by far the greatest number of adherents, especially in Korea and Japan were he is known as Amida. As Amida he presides over Sukhavati, a paradise for those who have reached salvation. Since he is a kindly lord, he freely admits to this paradise all those who truly seek the path of righteousness and call upon him for admittance. Some followers of Amida believe that simply repeating his name and calling upon him for salvation will grant them eternal bliss:

"Beings are not born in that Buddha's country as a reward and a result of good works performed in this present life. No, all men or women who hear and bear in mind for one, two, three, four, five, six or seven nights the name of Amida, when they come to die, Amida will stand before them in the hour of death, they will depart this life with quiet minds and after death they will be born in Paradise."[37]

His kindness and possibly his willingness to allow so many into paradise, had made him more popular in Korea and Japan than even Gautama himself.

How distant this is from Gautama's original concepts. Remember, he had specifically stated that prayers were useless and man could only be saved by his specific actions within any given cycle of transmigration. He had indicated that even the gods were subject to both Karma and samsara; they could not help mankind for they were equally subject to the laws of Being.

Yet with all the changes that have occurred during the evolution of Buddhism, most of the basic concepts of what constitutes a good and happy life remain constant::

Do not take life.
Do not steal.
Tell the truth.
Be generous and kind to all your fellow beings.
Be ethical and fair in all your dealings with others.
Show devotion and respect to your parents.
Show respect to your teachers.

Meditate in order to understand your own shortcomings
and what actions you must take in order to improve
yourself.

Material goods and power are meaningless in relation to
good deeds which are of the greatest significance
in achieving salvation, Nirvana or paradise.

Again, while the religion is vastly different from Christianity,
none can doubt the similarity in what constitutes a good and
happy life. Surely, no Christian teacher could hold that any of
these precepts went contrary to basic Christian principles. Let
us now look at a brief synopsis of Christian concepts concerning the journey to happiness and salvation.

Chapter 5 - Christianity

Christians are by definition those who believe in the Messiah. Judaism had preached the coming of a Messiah, the anointed one of God. Jesus Christ is this Messiah for Christians. The word Christ is derived from the Greek word *Christos*, meaning Messiah.[38]

Christians were originally a small sect within the religion of Judaism. In the beginning they observed many of the Jewish practices such as dietary laws, holding the Sabbath on Saturday, honoring the Holy Temple in Jerusalem, and celebrating many of the existing Jewish festivals. Unlike other Jews they believed that the Messiah was Jesus Christ; that He was the Son of God, who was crucified, and arose from the dead to sit at the right hand of God.

They also believed in a ritual immersion in water to cleanse the sins of those who had repented of their sins and turned to a new life. After baptism, Christians were allowed to participate in the communal meal ending in the taking of ritual bread and wine, the Eucharist or "thanksgiving." The bread represented the body of Christ, and the wine represented the blood of Christ. This was to remind all Christians of Christ's gift to them and his inevitable return. Sunday became the Lord's Day; the day His resurrection was commemorated.

Christians believed that Christ's suffering, or "Passion," death, and resurrection from the dead established a complete victory over sin and evil in the world. Christ would next come to earth to judge mankind and inaugurate the Kingdom of God.

These early Christians stood out from other religious groups due to their intense evangelizing both in and outside the Jewish community. Part of this was due to their belief that the end of the world and the return of Christ was near. They had to get the word to all who would listen before this occurred. The apostles of Jesus and many others believers became wandering teachers traveling throughout the Roman Empire from Asia Minor to Spain.

In the time of the early founders of the religion, taking in Gentiles was controversial. But just a few years later, the message of Jesus was being accepted far more widely by Gentiles than by Jews. Consequently many of the dietary laws and the requirement for circumcision were eliminated. Gradually during this period Christianity became a completely new religion separate from Judaism, rather than being a sect within the Jewish tradition.

The concept of the Holy Spirit also became an important part of Christianity during this period. The Holy Spirit was God's Manifestation on earth. God sent His Sprit to guide the church until the return of His Son, Jesus Christ. Eventually this developed into the Holy Trinity of God, Son and Holy Sprit. Since the Holy Spirit guided the church and its leaders, the activities of the church and its leaders were a manifestation of God's work here on earth.

In these early years of development the church began to organize along administrative lines of authority. The lowest priestly office, any office which necessitated the laying on of hands by a Bishop to indicate transmission of the Holy Spirit, became the deacon, who was responsible for managing established rituals within the church. Bishops were originally elected by the vote of all Christians within a community and only Bishops could perform the ritual of bread and wine. As the Christian community grew, it became impossible for the Bishop to perform this sacrament for all followers, and priests were ordained to both preach and celebrate the Eucharist.

During the first three centuries the New Testament was also written. The letters of Paul are the earliest Christian literature; next came the Gospels, telling the storey of the life of Jesus, and then Acts telling of the early apostles. The basic foundation of Christian religion was formulated during this time.

While Roman emperors had persecuted Christians, by 312 A.D. the new emperor Constantine actively supported the Christian church due to his belief that God had helped him during a crucial battle. While this did not bring on a massive number of converts, at the time even Constantine also supported pagan gods, it brought wealth and prestige to the church and great power to the bishops.

There were already schisms within the church during these first three centuries. One group diverging from church teachings was the Gnostics, from the Greek *gnosis* or knowledge. They believed they had special knowledge that did not come from church literature or teachings. Most Gnostics believed the world was created by an evil god and the true God was separate and apart from any material world and could only be known through mystical revelation. Marcion, a Gnostic leader from Asia Minor believed that we should remove the Old Testament from Christian writings because it was the work of the evil god who created the earth. Mani, who deemed himself an apostle of Jesus Christ, taught that the universe was divided into the forces of Dark and Light. He believed the God of Light had sent many messengers to earth and the most perfect of these was Jesus Christ. He taught that Jesus had only seemed to be human and material and that in reality He was divine and could not have suffered and died on the cross. His concept was that Jesus was a Savior for mankind, but His manifestation as a human was only an illusion. Mani had many followers including Augustine, who spent ten years as a Manichee. The majority of Christians, however, agreed that Jesus was both human and divine. This schism virtually disappeared by 600 A.D. in the western churches and by 1000 A.D. in the eastern.[39]

Another major controversy arose when Arius, a learned presbyter of Alexandria in the early fourth century, stated that Christ

was different from God and had been created by God. He believed that while Christ was more than human and an angelic
being, Christ was not God. Instead he reasoned that Christ was
more than human and an angelic principle of the cosmos, a view
that harkened back to classical Greek thought and the works of
Socrates and Plato. This was a great controversy for the church
since salvation through Christ was imperiled by this concept. If
Christ is only an angelic being and angelic beings can turn evil,
no salvation through Christ would be possible.

To deal with this schism, Constantine called the Council of
Nicea in 325 A.D. The council of bishops decided against the
views of Aruis, but the controversy took many years to be truly
resolved with Arius winning numerous converts including later
emperors to his cause. Eventually, however, the views of Arius
disappeared from the mainstream of Christian doctrine.

Another major event in the evolution of Christianity occurred in the fifth century when the church was charged with
being the prime mover in the decline of the Roman Empire.
Basically the accusations rested on the concept that Christianity
was a weak religion glorifying kindness and meekness in a world
where the empire faced pagan religious groups who not only
were not willing to turn the other cheek, but exalted brute force
and butchery. It was Augustine's response to such criticisms
that culminated in a great unification of church doctrine and
direction and propelled Christianity to become a major religion.

Augustine's great work *De Civitate Dei,* "On the City of God,"
argued that all human endeavors, including empires, are ephem-
eral possibilities that come and go with time; only the City of
God exists through eternity. All of man's material endeavors

are subject to corruption and fall back to the dust from which they came. Just as the Persian Empire had fallen, just as the Greek Empire had fallen, so would all others. He stated that such things were transitory and that only acting within the Christian faith and with Christian value and guarding the true church could mankind gain the only thing worth having – salvation.

It should be noted that Augustine believed in predestination which would itself cause some continuing controversy even to this day within the Christian faith. Augustine is stating that since God is all-knowing and all-powerful, He knows the fate of each human being, and consequently there is no true free will as all falls within that which God has ordained, and that which God already knows prior to any action, good or evil, taken by an individual man. No matter his position on predestination, much of which is actually more of a logical and philosophical conundrum, his *De Civitate Dei* did much to bring the principles of Christian thought to a focus within the community of the church.

The separation of Eastern Orthodox and Roman Catholic faiths had a far greater effect on Christianity than recondite concepts of predestination. By the sixth century, with an emperor of the western empire and an emperor of the eastern empire, with barbarian invasions threatening both empires; these two segments of the Christian church grew further and further apart. As the Roman Empire declined ever more rapidly, the eastern, or Byzantine Empire, remained stable for many centuries.

The pope in Rome continued to believe that he was the single guiding force for the Christian religion. The monarchs in the Byzantine Empire had far more direct interaction in church affairs than those of the former Roman Empire and held, in effect, a semi-priestly relationship to the church. In Rome the ruler was simply seen as a guardian of the church who had no other direct influence on church affairs. Byzantine monarchs had no reason to wish the patriarch of the East to be under the domination of the pope in Rome.

There were other differences between those two great counterweights of Christian faith. In the west there was a greater emphasis on perfection in ritual, the manifestation of dignity within all actions of the church, the need for sacrifice and purification from sin. All of mankind should seek perfection in their actions and beliefs that they may find salvation and such salvation cannot be achieved without discipline, order and humility.

While such concepts were not absent in the East, there was a greater emphasis on a mystical union with God; deification more than purification. Here the Eucharist was not just a matter of a cleansing of sin, it embodied a sharing of Christ's human and divine nature. It also allowed the church to reach up to the heavens to be touched by the holy assembly of saints as an adumbration of the return of Christ in the certain future. The East emphasized the transformation of being though immediate and personal contact with the divine. The West placed more emphasis on achieving perfection, and thus salvation, though absolute adherence to Christian doctrine and the utter acceptance of the immense debt owed to God.

The formal division of the Catholic and Orthodox churches is traditionally dated at 1054 A.D.[40] A Byzantine colony in southern Italy was attacked by the Normans and subjected to their rule. Pope Leo IX then demanded that the

Orthodox population change their allegiance to the pope in Rome. The Eastern patriarch, Michael Cerulatius, was not exactly pleased with this concept. When Pope Leo IX sent legates to Constantinople to make these demands, the patriarch dismissed them with scorn. The legates then went directly to the church of Saint Sophia and formally presented a bull of excommunication against Cerularius, obviously previously formulated by the pope for this eventuality. Cerularius then communed a council of bishops and formally excommunicate the legates. With the crusaders' attack on Constantinople in 1204 A.D., relations between East and West were severed. After this, the Orthodox Church was shattered into numerous national divisions – Greek Orthodox, Russian Orthodox and the many others that now exist with their own patriarchs.

The work of Thomas Aquinas, also in the thirteenth century, had a far more rewarding effect on Christianity. With the return of Greek concepts and ideas through the translations of Arabic copies of Greek philosophers found in Toledo after its conquest by Christians, numerous ideological conflicts appeared between Christian scholars. Concepts such as the belief that matter need have no prime mover any more than a prime mover would have to have a prime mover, or man was only part of a single mind that simply appeared in an illusory form, or that God was impersonal and would destroy his creation just as easily as he had created it produced a furor against the new Aristotelian logic and might well have driven Christianity, and Western culture into a fanatical animosity towards all kinds of knowledge and science.

Aquinas, however, used Aristotelian logic to prove the doctrines of the church. His *Summa Theologica*, "Comprehensive Theology," provided a foundation for Roman Catholic doctrine. One of Aquinas' most important arguments concerned the predestination concepts of Augustine that we have previously discussed. While Augustine had emphasized the utter dependence of man on God's grace, the baseness of human nature and a dualism of body and spirit, Aquinas attempted to unite the two as working in harmony towards salvation. Aquinas maintained that the material and spiritual were interrelated rather than standing in opposition to one another.

Aquinas stated that human reason and man himself had been made in the image of God. While both human nature and human reason were flawed by sin, through God's grace man could achieve perfection and reach salvation within God. God's grace is the vehicle by which man can be carried into cooperation with God's great design for the universe. The material and the spiritual exist in harmony within God's grand universe of Being. This effect of Aquinas' arguments had monumental consequences in that they prevented a dichotomy within the church.

By the fourteenth century the harmony between political corruption and greed within the church were becoming as well known as Aquinas. The stability of European society had also been greatly affected by the Hundred Years' War (1337-1453) and the Black Death, which began in 1348 and killed one third of Europe's population.[41]

During the Hundred Years' War, the papacy had allied itself with France and moved the seat of papal control from Rome to Avignon. There were two popes, one in Rome and one in Avigon. This issue was further complicated when the Council of Pisa declared the heresy of both popes and elected a third. While there had certainly been corruption and political intrigue within the papacy prior to this, the effect of these machinations on the masses was profound. It is difficult to believe in the authority of someone whose word is law, when that person can be replaced within the blink of an eye by another council of cardinals.

The papal business in indulgences further eroded the sanctity of the papal office and of the church. Originally an indulgence, a papal decree granting a person remission from punishment in purgatory, could only be granted based on a spiritual service to God and the church, such as services provided by the crusaders. By the fifteenth century Pope Sixtus IV was selling indulgences for the dead; a living relative could simply pay a fee, and his dead relative would be released from the pain of purgatory.[42]

Church offices were also sold. Many priests and bishops were openly living with concubines. They could be absolved of their sins by paying a concubine fee, and if they fathered a child, they could pay a "cradle fee." In short, corruption permeated the Roman Catholic Church and reformers knew that some action must be taken in order to save the sanctity of the church.

In Florence Savonarola, a Dominican friar, spoke out vehemently against the rampant corruption. Erasmus wrote numerous works detailing the corruption of the church and the need for reform. In Germany, Martin Luther dramatically confronted the church with his demands for reforms. It was Martin Luther's declarations against corruption and statements of reform that sparked the Protestant Reformation. It should be noted that Martin Luther did not initially wish to form a separate church; his real goal was to reform the existing church.

The rise of the middle class greatly influenced the demand for a new church. Lay citizens had tired of vast church holdings going untaxed and church officials forming an elite caste outside of all other professions. Protestant reformers insisted that all professions were "callings" and that there was no special designation by God as to the holiness of church officials.

Martin Luther in Germany and Ulrich Zwingli and John Calvin in Switzerland also assailed the worth and merit of monastic orders. They put forth the "priesthood of all believers," which meant that every Christian was in charge of his or her own journey to salvation. Mankind did not need an intermediary, priest, to reach towards God.

The reformists especially attacked the concept of the priest as confessor. By the fifteenth century penance had become an incredibly complex system with the priest cataloguing a long list of major and minor sins and accompanying penance for each church member. Every church member had to remember every sin and be aware of every type of possible sin within church directives. The reformists eliminated the need for the priest as confessor by stating that any Christian could confess to any other Christian, and that in this sense all Christians were priests.

The sacraments of extreme unction and penance were eliminated along with monastic vows. Other penances such as pilgrimages to the Holy Land and the monetary endowment of masses were removed from church doctrine.

The numerous high masses of the Roman Catholic Church disappeared in favor of celebrations of the Lord's Supper. Most of the reformers denied that Christ's body was actually present in the mass of the Eucharist; the Lord's Supper was a memorial to Christ, not that his actual presence was in the bread and wine. Martin Luther however continued to hold that Christ was actually present within the reality of the bread and wine.

The teachings of "the Word," the Holy Scriptures, replaced the many sacraments of the Roman Catholic Church. One became one with God "through grace by faith alone". By preaching the Word to the assembled Christians, and their acceptance of the Word, mankind was led to the path of salvation, *sola fide, sola scriptura* – by faith alone, by Scripture alone.[43]

With the impetus of Martin Luther in Germany and Ulrich Zwingli and John Calvin in Switzerland, these two countries rapidly became centers of Protestant reform. In England, Henry VIII was denied an annulment for one of his many marriages; and he annulled his country's relation with the Roman Catholic Church. In 1534 the king issued the Act of Supremacy which declared him to be the king of England and the head of the Church of England. When Queen Elizabeth came to power in 1559, she gradually established the Reformation that created the Church of England, which later in America would become the Episcopal Church.

The majority of the Christian denominations evolved from those beginnings. Lutheran churches came from Martin Luther's reforms. The Reformed churches – German, Dutch and others – were based on the teachings of Calvin and Zwingli. When Calvinism reached England it became the

Puritan movement that attempted to purify the Church of England. From this Puritan doctrine came Presbyterian, Congregationalist, Baptist, and Quaker churches. In the eighteenth century another reformation within the Church of England produced the Methodist church.

The Mennonite church was founded in the 1500's when it broke away from the Zurich state church. The Bible is the sole basis of faith and beliefs are outlined in the Dordrecht Confession of Faith. Mennonites shun ostentation, worldly ways, and all modern innovation. The sacraments are adult baptism and communion.

The Lutheran church is based on the principles of Martin Luther and the Augsburg Confession, 1530. Central to their beliefs is the concept that salvation comes through faith alone. The first Presbyterian Church was founded by John Knox in Scotland in 1557. All their faith is based on the complete accuracy of the scriptures. There are two sacraments, baptism and communion. The church structure is organized into a series of directing counsels consisting of lay members, presbyters, and clergy. The first Presbyterian church was founded by John Smyth in England in 1609, and in America the first Baptist church was established in Rhode Island in 1638.

In the seventeenth century in England George Fox founded the Religious Society of Friends, Quakers. He professed a doctrine of Inner Light, the voice of God's Holy Spirit. This Inner Light can only come from the individual and cannot be learned from the preaching of others. Quaker services are characterized by quite group meditation without sermons or rituals. Quakers believe in the total sanctity of human life and will not bear arms or take oaths binding them to bear arms. They are active in peace movements and social welfare.

The Episcopal Church broke with the Church of England and elected its first bishop, Samuel Seabury, in 1784. The Book of Common Prayer and an interpretation of scripture based on modifications of the Thirty-Nine Articles of the Church of England form the basis of worship.

The Reverend John Wesley, an evangelist within the Church of England established his own Wesleyan Methodist Church in 1738. The Methodist Episcopal Church was founded in America in 1784. As the name indicates religion should be studied by "rule and method," and the Bible should be interpreted both by tradition and reason. Communion and the baptism of both adults and infants are practiced.

The Unitarian Universal Association was created in 1779 by the merger of the Universal Church of America and the American Unitarian Association. Members profess no creed and theist, and humanists and agnostics are accepted in religious fellowship. Their beliefs center around ethical and humanitarian concerns and their goal is a worldwide interfaith religious community.

The Church of Christ was organized by Presbyterians in Kentucky in 1804 and in Pennsylvania in 1809. The New Testament is accepted as the basis of faith without any elaboration. Only adults are baptized.

The Mormon religion, Church of Jesus Christ of Latter-day Saints, was founded by Joseph Smith in 1831. The church beliefs are based on the *Book of Mormon*, other writings by Joseph Smith, and *The Pearl of Great Price*. Emphasis is placed on revelation through the connection of spiritual and physical worlds and through proselytizing. Members abstain from alcohol, tobacco, and all substances seen as changing or impairing conscious thought. Sacraments are baptism for adults, the laying on of hands and communion.

Jehovah's Witnesses was founded by Charles T. Russell in the late nineteenth century. Members' believe in the imminent second coming of Christ. All members of the church are ministers who believe that one of the most important vehicles of faith and salvation is to bring the world of God to others by door-to-door missionary work. They refuse service in the armed forces, refuse to salute flags, will not accept transfusions, will not participate in government, and consider smoking, drinking, dancing and card playing inappropriate for those desiring salvation.

In this same era the Seventh-Day Adventist church was founded by Ellen G. White. This was a millennial sect believing in the thousand-year reign of Christ over the earth before the destruction of the devil and sinners leading to the City of God upon the earth. Seventh-Day Adventist also believe that the gift of prophecy is given to some of God's chosen, such as Ellen G. White. Emphasis is placed on the human body as temple of the Holy Spirit; consequently we must exercise, have an appropriate diet and avoid tobacco, alcohol and all drugs. The seventh day that God rested is celebrated from dawn to dawn because the Holy Spirit is considered to be especially prevalent in reaching out to mankind, since this is the day God specifically assigned for the intensity of this communion.

Pentecostal churches emerged from the "holiness movement" among Methodist and some other Protestant denominations in the early twentieth century. The Assemblies of God are the largest Pentecostal group. Speaking in tongues, a belief in the imminent second coming of Jesus, and faith healing are articles of faith. Their sacraments are adult baptism and communion.[45]

The Roman Catholic Church made significant changes in the twentieth century. During this period there was a great deal of opposition amongst clergy and layman concerning the refusal of the church to adopt more modern and moderate attitudes and church directives. In response to these increasingly vehement criticisms, the Second Vatican Council (1962-1965) was convened by Pope John XXIII. The council adopted directives supporting religious freedoms and accepting Protestant religions. Previous to this Protestants had been considered heretics and more importantly, beyond God's salvation. Mass was translated from Latin into the language of the religious community being served. The long liturgies were limited in order to provide more time for sermons and congregational singing.

Across all these many denominations of the Christian faith, the majority of core beliefs in what constitutes a good and happy life remain constant. These beliefs appear both in the Ten Commandments and in the body of faith held by most Christian churches:

Honor thy father and mother.
Thou shalt not kill.
Thou shalt not commit adultery.

Thou shalt not steal.

Thou shalt not bear false witness.

Thou shalt not covet anything that is thy neighbor's.

Do unto others as you would have them do unto you.

Be generous in the giving of charity to others.

Do not judge lest you be judged.

Material wealth is unimportant in achieving salvation.

You are known by the good works that you do for others.

We are responsible for our thoughts and deeds.

Chapter 6 - Concepts Across Religions

When you realize the vast differences between Hinduism, Buddhism, and Christianity, it is amazing the similarities that exist in their core concepts concerning the living of a good and happy life. While there are startling differences in dogma, there are few differences in the directions for how to act towards others, the sanctity of family life, the importance of loyalty to family and friends, the need to do good deeds, the need for charity to others, the importance of not judging and deriding others, the necessity for treating all beings with dignity, the importance of filial love and devotion, the importance of always acting in an ethical manner in all aspects of your life, and the lack of importance of worldly treasure in obtaining salvation or happiness. Cross-referencing the postulates of these three diverse religions to identify concepts of a good and happy life which appear in each reveals the following:

Do not take human life.

Do not cheat or bear false witness.

Be generous and charitable to others.

Show respect to your parents.

Good deeds are a major component in the path to salvation.

Each of us bears responsibility for our actions.

Material wealth is unimportant in comparison to the value of the acts of kindness we give to others.

Do not humiliate others and respect the sanctity of all life.

The majority of directives concerning our behavior to one another and our responsibility to society are the same in all three religions. This recipe for a good and happy life has been developed over 3500 years by diverse cultures and ethnic groups. It has stood the test of time and changed little in the evolution of the religions we have reviewed.

Chapter 7 - Development of Psychology

By at least the sixth century B.C. the concept of examining the workings of the human mind begin to appear in India, China, and Greece. Confucius is quoted as stating, "A man can command his principles; principles do not master the man." The idea is important because it denotes control over "the mind." The words etched in stone at the Temple of Apollo are, "Know thyself." For the first time in recorded history, we see a distinction between the immediacy of what we are thinking at a given moment and the concept of a "mind" at work.

Scholars began to try to fathom how the mind worked and the meaning of life itself in the light of reflective thought. The

Hellenic period in Greece produced an astounding panorama of learned individuals dedicated to examining virtually every modern arena of psychology and philosophy. Prior to this period the word *psyche* referred to the immediacy of thoughts within an instant of time, not an entity holding memories, thoughts, hopes, fears, dreams, and some form of self-control over the workings of the entity. Aristotle was the first to use the term psyche as indicative of a step-by-step mental process that could be analyzed.[45] This is a vast change in direction, an identification of a process as an entity; it would lead to some of the greatest concepts in Western thought. As many scholars agree, probably no period in our history produced such an explosion of inquiry and knowledge.[46]

Prior to Aristotle, Alcmaeon posited that all knowledge and thought were derived from the information provided by our senses. Alcmaeon was, in a manner of speaking, the first Behaviorist. Protagoras saw a large problem with this concept – that all truth, logic and reason were based on knowledge coming form our senses. His famous quote, "Man is the measure of all things," alludes to an individual's interpretation of the information coming from his sense receptors.[47] Protagoras foreshadows all of the battles that have been fought in psychology and philosophy concerning whether or not there is a single truth to be known; and whether or not the truth is based solely on what can be seen, heard, tasted and felt.

Protagoras stated that knowledge is affected by both the amount of knowledge one is able to acquire and the age of the individual; knowledge was not a simple acceptance of data from the sense organs, but depended on an individual's abilities to interpret such data. The concept of a body, mind and psyche appear for the first time as an explanation for how human beings experience the world around them.

Psyche becomes the entity that binds together the three parts of the human equation. The words *arête*, human excellence, and *kalokagathia*, admirable good, appear during this period to denote the goals that each of us should attempt to reach.[48] There is more to life than the simple acceptance of stimuli from the world that surrounds us. Each of us in a room may receive the same information concerning an event, some will act based on the highest ideals of ethics and morality while others will act in such a manner as to deny these ideals. Each of us in a situation may receive the same information from the senses, but this does not mean that we will interpret the data in the same way or that we will act in accordance with any concept of excellence in human affairs. It is amazing to realize that these concepts were being argued in 480 B.C.

By 450 B.C. Hippocrates was attempting to change superstitious concepts concerning the causes of mental illness and substitute a theory of internal causation to explain bizarre or inappropriate behavior. It was not bad winds, or bad gods causing such thought processes, but something internal to the mind itself:

"Men ought to know that from the brain, and the brain only, arise our pleasures, joys, laughter, and jests as well as our sorrows, pains, grief, and tears."[49]

Hippocrates posited that there were four humors which composed all matter, and their balance within the brain accounted for well-being. An imbalance in these humors accounted for mental illness. While his four humor theory obviously is incorrect, it should be noted that when one changes the humors to such neuro-transmitters as serotonin, and acetylcholine, we have a very modern concept in psychology. Imbalances in neuro-transmitters drastically affect the workings of the mind, and a large body of scientific literature over the past fifty years demonstrates this beyond question. The most important concept, however, is the realization that the causative factors exist within the brain itself and are dependent on the functioning of this entity, not on mysterious, unknown causative factors beyond human control.

Socrates also believed that the mind functioned based on internal causative factors, not external determinations sent by gods or other mysterious beings. He conjectured, however, that all knowledge was present in our minds at birth and our goal should be the retrieval of this knowledge into the conscious mind. Socrates posited the existence of an immortal soul that did not die when the body died, but lived on forever. For him, knowledge was innate since we had lived before and would live many lives afterwards. True knowledge, according to Socrates, came form uncovering innate truths present in all of us. Through reasoning we can uncover the truth, not through the experiences of the senses which may, or may not provide any level of truth. This is the basis of his dialectical methods. He led his pupils to truths they already knew, in his belief, by working them through a path leading them to "find" the truth already existing in their minds. In many ways Socrates founded the division between mind and body, mind and soul.

It is important to note that Socrates placed great emphasis on leading a moral life as being the essence of the "good life." He admonished his followers to be kind, generous, honest, and ethical and to demonstrate moderation and tolerance in all aspects of their lives. He took no payments for his teachings and remained poor all his life though he could have been a rich man if he had accepted pay for his teachings. He is reported to have said upon seeing all the many expensive things in the marketplace of Athens, "How many things there are that I do not want."[50]

Plato was a pupil of Socrates for some eight years. He revered his teacher and much of the work he produced mirrors the thoughts of Socrates. Plato took many of these concepts far beyond Socrates, however, the dualism of the mind and spirit that we saw in all three of the religions reviewed now appears at a high level of philosophical argument in the works of Plato:

"The body fills us full of loves and lusts and fears and fancies of all kinds. We are slaves to the body's service. If we would have true knowledge of anything we must be quit of the body – the soul in herself must behold things in themselves; then we shall attain the wisdom we desire, be pure and have converse with the pure. And what is purification but the separation of the soul from the body."[51]

Plato sees truth only in the reality of concepts and abstract ideas. The information gained directly from the senses is without real merit. As Socrates before him, Plato saw knowledge as recollecting what we had already learned, but his work on perception and the development of "concepts" foreshadowed modern investigations into the same phenomenon.

Plato also foreshadowed Freud with his concept that the soul inhabiting a body works on three levels: thought or reason, spirit or will, and appetite or desire. He indicated while reason should have overall control, it should not dominate the others to such an extent that none of the three can function; there must be harmony among all. In the *Phaedrus* he likens the three to a chariot pulled by two horses, one lively but obedient (the spirit), and one violent and unruly (desire) with both managed by a charioteer (reason). This is amazingly similar to Freud's superego, ego, and id:

"When the reasoning and taming and ruling power of the personality is asleep, the wild beast within us, gorged with meat and drink, starts up having shaken off sleep, goes forth to satisfy desire; and there is no conceivable folly or crime – not excepting incest or parricide or the eating of forbidden food – which at such a time, when he is parted company with all shame and sense, a man may not be ready to commit."[52]

Plato discusses one of the most central concepts of psychology, the drive to be united with an eternal life force. He uses it to designate the drive to be untied with the loved one. Plato does not mean erotic love, but the love of the eternal, the perfect form or ideal that the person represents.

Aristotle, a pupil of Socrates, was born in Stagira in northern Greece in 384 B.C. While a pupil of Socrates, Aristotle's work emphasized a reliance on sense data in coordination with reason as the basis for all scientific study. He produced some one hundred and seventy works during his sixty-two years of life. While Plato was an Idealist, Aristotle was a Realist.[53]

Aristotle wrote that the mind was not the brain; it was the steps taken in the process of thinking and being aware of the stimuli around you. This mirrors all modern concepts of the cogitative process and information theory some 2000 years before the advent of any kind of scientific equipment capable of examining the process itself.

He indicated that our senses bring us perceptions of the world and the mind, and through deductive or inductive reasoning assigns these to categories based on shared qualities. Totally differing from his mentor Plato, he did not believe that we came into the world with knowledge that we simply had to recall. He believed the process involved perception, memory and reasoning which formed general concepts and ideas. This is an astonishingly accurate portrayal of the process as is his general concept of memory itself:

"When we try to recollect something, we experience certain antecedent movement, memories, until finally we come to the one after which customarily appears the one we seek. This is why we hunt up the series, having started in thought either from present intuition of some other and from something either similar or contrary to what we seek, or else from that which is contiguous to it."[54]

This is an extremely accurate portrayal of the real process based only on speculation and conjecture. In a manner of speaking, Aristotle was the father of modern cognitive theory.

There is little to note in the evolution of psychology between the times of the great Aristotle and Augustine, the Christian Aristotle, in the fourth century A.D. While we have previously discussed Augustine's masterpiece *The City of God*, his famous *Confessions* is more important in measuring his contribution to psychology.

Augustine was born in 354 A.D. in Tagaste, a town in what is now Algeria. His mother Monica was a Christian and his father Patricus was a pagan. Augustine lived a life of luxury within the dying Roman Empire. His *Confessions* detail his early years spent in debauchery. His readings in Greek philosophy and early Christian writings later led him to analyze much of his early behavior. In 387 A.D. Augustine had an epiphany after reading a passage from the writings of Saint Paul and was baptized into the church by Bishop Ambrose, later Saint Ambrose.

Augustine does a quite remarkable job of analyzing the reasons behind his own past behavior. He admits that he decided to commit sinful acts due to a lack of appropriate will power and ignorance of the truth concerning what creates a good and happy life. He divides the mind into a united trinity of memory, reason and will:

"Since these three memories, reason and will, are not three lives but one life, nor three minds but one mind, it follows that they are not three substances. These three are one, in that they are one life, one mind, one essence. But they are three, in that I remember that I have memory and understanding and will; and I understand that I understand and will and remember; and I will that I will and remember and understand. And therefore, while each as a whole is equal to each as a whole and each as a whole to all as whole, the three are one, one life, one mind and one essence."[55]

Augustine is addressing a problem that still plagues modern psychology. Who is it that remembers and wills and understands? How can one mind be both within an active thought process and reflecting simultaneously upon itself? When an act of will occurs to stop an impulsive and inappropriate action, who is acting on whom to stop the action?

Aristotle, Augustine and other great thinkers we have reviewed established the basis of the most crucial questions within psychology. The actual birth of psychology as a science is normally dated at 1879, however. This was the period when Wilhelm Wundt began pioneering scientific experiments in perception and reaction times at the University of Leipzig. Experimental psychology became a reality applicable to the study of the mental process itself:

"The importance that experimentation will eventually have in psychology can hardly be visualized to its full extent as yet. It has often been held that the area of sensation and perception is the only one in which the use of experimental method is possible, but surely this is a prejudice. As soon as psyche is viewed as a natural phenomenon, and psychology as a natural science,

the experimental methods must also be capable of full applica-
tion to this science."[56]

The experimental methods developed by Wundt form the basis
of all modern experimental psychology. Wundt brought back
the concept of trying to understand the complex workings of
the human mind that had been the cornerstone of the great
thinkers from early Greek philosophy and Christian theology,
and added experimental methods to the process.

From the experimental methods of Wundt to a back to the
future introspection and conjecture method appears with the
work of Sigmund Freud. Freud was born in 1856 in Freiberg, a
small town in Moravia. He was the son of a poor, itinerant
Jewish trader in woolens, cloth, hides and farm produce. Through
extraordinary hard work Freud became a medical student and
graduated from the University of Vienna. His actual goal after
college was to work as a physiologist and do only pure research.[57]

Freud gave up this dream because as a Jew the likelihood of
his being able to make a living in such an enterprise was extremely low, and the world of psychology had changed. In 1886
Freud opened a practice in neurological and brain disorders. He
accepted referrals of patients with hysterical disorders only because he needed the money.

He developed his concepts of "free association" at the direction of one of his patients. Baroness Fanny Moser, a forty-
year old widow, suffered from facial tics, hallucinations of writh-
ing snakes and dead rats. She also suffered from dreams concerning vultures and fierce wild animals, frequent interruption
of her speech by a spastic clacking or popping noise which she

made by rapidly opening and closing her mouth, and a fear of socializing and a hatred of strangers. In a session in which the Baroness complained of gastric pains, Freud asked her why she thought she was experiencing these pains:

"Her answer, which she gave rather grudgingly, was that she did not know. I requested her to remember by tomorrow. She then said in a definitely grumbling tone that I was not to keep on asking her where this or that had come from, but to let her tell me what she had to say."[58]

Freud took her at her word and she was right. This method of free association allowed the patient to ramble on until hidden memories and insights appeared as if by magic from this conglomeration of apparently unrelated memories. Freud began to "analyze" the chain of associations which led to pathogenic ideas which were causing the hysterical symptoms. He published his first work on "analysis" in 1896, *Studies*.

Freud later developed his concept of transference from analyzing patient's dreams. Dream interpretation became the second major element in his process of analysis when he realized that dreams, when interpreted by analysis, showed that feelings concerning important people in his patients' lives were being transferred to him. He then decided that transference was essential in the therapy process if the patients were truly to be able to "work through" their pathogenic thinking.

Freud ruthlessly analyzed his own dreams and the workings of his conscious mind. From these and his analysis of patients, Freud developed his concepts of childish fantasies leading to pathogenic thinking in the adult and the idea of childhood sexuality. This was extremely dangerous material for the time, but Freud published his findings and beliefs nevertheless.

Freud was delving into the unconscious mind, a place were other scientists had tread before only as a mystical possibility. The concept of the unconscious mind was not actually developed by Freud; Leibniz, William James, poets and philosophers had postulated its existence. Most of these had only considered the unconscious to be a repository of experiences waiting to be recalled. Freud labeled this the "preconscious."

Freud maintained that the mind had three levels of functioning; the conscious, the preconscious, and the unconscious. For Freud the unconscious was not a warehouse for inactive, unused memory; it was a world unto itself consisting of powerful primitive drives and forbidden desires that constantly generated pressure on the conscious mind, albeit in a disguised and altered form, thereby motivating and determining elements of our behavior.[59]

The unconscious mind, for Freud, is not just a place where dangerous ideas or desires are hidden; it is the home of primary drive states – a life force.

Later Freud would develop these concepts into the tripartite psyche. He postulated that the mind consisted of an id, an ego, and a superego. He did not see these as entities, but as names of clusters working within the mental process to serve different and necessary functions for the stability of the person.

For newborn children, Freud believed that all processes were id processes, unconscious and primary. There is no function of reason, only instinctual demands and primitive drive states essential to self-preservation: hunger, thirst, sexuality and aggression. The id works only on the pleasure principle; it avoids all that gives pain and accepts all that gives pleasure; it seeks the relief from drive states without any consideration of the consequences to others. It is without conscience, only pleasure and pain matter.[60]

Obviously, a being possessing only an id would have some difficulty living in society. Child rearing and socialization allows for control of the id and its demands for immediate need gratification. Part of this child rearing is based on the pleasure-pain principle that the child will learn impulse control, if by learning impulse control greater rewards will occur and less pain endured. During this period of childhood the ego begins to form.

The ego, which actually overlaps and merges with the id, is capable of conscious thought and reason. This is not just a reaction to the pleasure-pain principle; the ego is capable of learning these concepts and can engage in independent thought. Much of the ego's process thinking, however, is in the preconscious — not repressed, but not within the immediacy of conscious thought. When solutions to problems seem to pop into our head for no apparent reason, it is because we have been working on the problem beneath the level of the conscious mind. The preconscious operates many of the actions we repeat day in and day out so that the conscious mind can use its limited resources elsewhere. The concert pianist does not consciously think of the placement of every finger on the keyboard for every note. When you are writing, you do not consciously think of the necessary angle of the pen to achieve each letter.

The superego is the repository of all the ethical and moral principles we ingest in childhood. The superego is unconscious, but governs actions within the conscious mind. The repetition of commands such as "you must not" or "you should" or "you must" are transformed by identification with the powerful figures in childhood to "I must not" or "I should" or "I must" commands. Moral values and ethical ideas are internalized through this process.[61]

There is a balance between the ego and the superego. The ego may decide that something is in its best immediate interest, but may be overridden by the superego. A starving man may feel, ego drive, that he must save all his food for himself, but the superego insists that food be shared because it is a prime directive learned in childhood.

Another major contribution to psychology made by Freud was his interpretation of "instinct." He did not mean the imprints of knowledge necessary to allow spiders to spin their webs without going to school. His *instinct* refers to a drive or moving force. Originally he concentrated on sexual drives and the general drive to maintain and sustain the individual life. Work with "repetition compulsions" and the horrors of World War I led him to believe that there was a drive to destroy or aggress.

From these conjectures he developed the concept that there were two major opposing drive forces: the life instinct, or Eros, and the death instinct, or Thanatos. Thanatos represented all impulses toward hostility, sadism, and aggression.[62]

From these ideas he developed the "displacement theory." Desired actions that cannot be acted upon due to overriding fear of retribution become neurotic symptoms. While these symptoms may be costly to the individual, they are not perceived as being less costly than the alternative direct expression. Displacement is a kind of defense mechanism for the ego.

Freud developed ideas concerning a number of defense mechanisms that are crucial in understanding human behavior. He saw "denial" as the most primitive defense mechanism. A smoker may deny that there is any real evidence linking lung cancer to smoking, a cancer victim may deny that the cancer is terminal against all evidence to the contrary.

"Rationalization" is a more intricate and sophisticated form of denial. In rationalizations we form convoluted explanations which explain our denial of a reality. We refuse to help someone because it would only make them suffer more in the long run and they have to learn for themselves. A battered woman stays with her husband because she loves him and knows that he actually needs her and will soon stop his abuse no matter how many times this is proved wrong. A person did not really steal the watch because it was laying out in the open; it was lost and needed to be found by someone. You would have remembered to take a needed action, but there were just too many competing demands on your time when you simply did not wish to take the action.

"Reaction formation" pulls the problem inside out. A person loving pornography may become the most vehement opponent of any type of sexual expression. An individual who fears homosexual desires may become the most rabid vilifier of homosexual behavior. The individual displays an exaggerated stance exactly opposite to that which he fears to possess.

In "intellectualization" an individual takes an ostensibly intellectual interest in what he would otherwise consider unacceptable. Someone with sadistic drives may become a social scientist specializing in the study of sadism and sadists, and their victims. A person who enjoys pornography may become the head of the censor board.

"Projection" attributes one's own unacceptable thoughts, actions or desires to others. People who have racial prejudices may attribute the holding of racial prejudices to members of the other race. Individuals who commit fraud in order to obtain wealth may attribute these desires to others whom they find as easy targets due to lower social status or higher social status.

"Sublimation" is the defense mechanism most beneficial to society. In sublimation, some instinctual demand is altered into a socially acceptable action. Surgeons get to cut into people every day and hold a noble profession. Exhibitionists make excellent writers and painters since their base desire is transferred into an art form. Sadistic impulses can be vented in professional sports with attendant prestige, power and wealth.

Freud's work was monumental because it again opened psychology to the science of introspection and learned conjecture. His contribution was well summed up by the historian of psychology L. S. Heanshaw:

"Freud brought psychologists face to face with the whole range of human problems, with the central questions that had been treated by great thinkers, artists, and writers from ancient times, but had been almost excluded from academic schools – with problems of love and hate, of happiness and misery; with

the turmoil of social discontent and violence, as well as the tri-
fling errors and slips of everyday existence; with the towering
edifices of religious belief as well as the petty, but tragic, ten-
sions of family life."[63]

While Freud led psychology into the depth of introspection, another major leap in psychological concepts occurred with
Edward Lee Thorndike (1874-1947) and his laws of natural learning – behaviorism. Thorndike was the son of a Methodist min-
ister and graduated from Wesleyan University with the highest
grade average in fifty years. He studied under William James at
Harvard and James Cattel at Columbia University.[64]

Thorndike did not have the Baroness Fanny Moser for a
muse and instead worked with chickens, cats, and dogs. While
there had been concepts concerning the pleasure-pain principle
for decades, there had been no real concept of how specific
behaviors were learned. Was higher order reasoning necessary
for an animal to learn behavior or was some other mechanism at
work? Thorndike believed that higher order reasoning was not
necessary for animals to learn. When he put a chicken in a maze,
it got better at finding its way out of the maze with increased
levels of trials:

"The chick, when confronted by loneliness and confining
walls, responds by those acts which in similar situations in nature would be likely to free him. Some one of these acts leads
him to the successful act, and the resulting pleasure stamps it in.
Absence of pleasure stamps all others out."[65]

Behavioral psychology is considered to be founded in this simple statement. Thorndike ran thousands of closely controlled experiments on different types of animals.

He distilled his findings into a theory of "connectionism" which could be expressed in two laws. The first law he named the Law of Effect. Basically this states that the effect of any given action determines the likelihood that it will be the response in the face of a given stimulus. Behavior that is rewarded or "reinforced" is maintained in the face of the same stimulus and behavior that is not reinforced ceases, or has a higher likelihood of ceasing.

The second law is the Law of Exercise. A response to a given stimulus will be more strongly connected to that stimulus in relation to the increase in the number of times the connection occurs and the duration of that connection. The number of times a behavior is reinforced in response to a given stimulus, and the greater the reinforcing value, the greater the likelihood the behavior will occur when the stimulus is presented. While this may seem simple learning theory now, it had never been formulated in such terms prior to Thorndike's work.

Clark L. Hull (1884-1952) took Thorndike's work to a much higher degree of sophistication. His goal was to make behaviorism a quantitatively exact science modeled after Newtonian physics.[66]

While he began with the extent concepts of stimulus-response (S-R) which Thorndike had advanced, Hull postulated numerous intervening factors involved in the process. The level of a given drive state is paramount to the number of behaviors and the intensity of the behaviors. A hungry chicken will work a lot longer and more intensely than a satiated chicken if the reward for a behavior is only food. The next variable was the strength of the reinforcement – amount of food, reduction of fear. Other variables include the number of times the stimulus has previously been paired with the reinforcer, the level of drive reduction (level of satiation involved in the difference between the level of the drive state and its reduction), the length of time between one pairing of the stimulus and response, and the level of fatigue of the subject. Hull did an incredible amount of research and many of his theories are valid, but his attempts to quantify all behavior in a general field theory failed. The complexity of human behavior was simply beyond the reach of Newtonian physics. The father of behaviorism died in relative obscurity in 1952.

The next important behaviorist B. F. Skinner became the best known psychologist in the world. Skinner was a showman who delighted in entertaining and irritating both the public and members of his profession.

Skinner's goal was to determine how human behavior is created by external stimuli. His learning theory, he claimed, simply stated that everything we do and are is determined by our history of rewards and punishments. He stated that he did not believe that a person was either free or responsible. Basically we are the sum of what has happened to us in the past and our original genetic possibilities.

Skinner taught that any possibility within a given being's repertoire of responses can be conditioned in the face of any stimulus. He taught pigeons how to peck out tunes on a toy piano and to play a type of table tennis with their beaks. These were widely seen on television and amazed the public. The basic concept, however, is a simple one. The pigeon will engage in general pigeon behavior while in a confined space with a piano and a tray into which the observer can drop food without being seen by the pigeon. At some time the pigeon will come near the piano and a food pellet will fall in the tray. The pigeon will connect proximity to the piano to receiving food. Pecking behavior is natural to the pigeon, and soon he will peck a key on the piano and receive an increased level of food. Then food will be withheld until the pigeon pecks a desired key. Soon food will be withheld until the beginning of a series of keys is pecked in the order desired. Within a relatively short period of time, the pigeon will be able to play the desired tune consistently.

This type of training involves important elements of behavioral theory developed by Skinner. The pigeon is being "shaped" towards the desired goal through a series of "successive approximations" of the target goal. Each step involves an element essential to the final behavior – the pigeon pecks the piano, he pecks a key starting a sequence of the tune, he pecks two keys in the desired sequence. At each stage there is "differential reinforcement;" for some actions he receives higher level rewards, for some no rewards and for some only decreased rewards. At the final stages of training, when the pigeon has mastered the task and is repeating it, a "partial reinforcement" paradigm is adopted—food pellets are delivered after the behavior sometimes and sometimes they are not delivered and sometimes there is a delayed delivery. This vastly increases the likelihood that the pigeon will continue the behavior, and increase the intensity and number of behaviors, with decreasing reinforcement once the behavior is learned. This is the type of reinforcement that occurs on a slot-machine, and makes casinos rich.

For all of his emphasis on humans being the sum of experiences and genetics, Skinner's real desires appear in his cult classic, *Walden Two*. He envisions a utopia with a small society where children are taught from birth onward to be cooperative and sociable. They are of course taught these skills through Skinnerian conditioning. Only positive reinforcement, and never punishment, is used to shape the child's behavior towards the intended goals – the good and happiness of all. Skinner wants a world in which people are good and kind to one another; a world in which all brutality and humiliation are erased, a world in which the primary goal is to insure the happiness of others.

We have taken a rapid trip through the evolution of psychology with emphasis on experimental psychology, psychoanalytical theory, and behaviorism. Each of the schools of thought places emphasis on vastly different aspects of the human mind and human experience. There are virtually no differences in their modern interpretations of what is and what is not mental illness. All accept the concept that our actions are based on both internal and external events. All see the mind as a singularity with different areas of the mind providing differing functions to maintain the well-being of the individual. Each searches for the causative factors of human happiness and misery.

It would initially appear that their criteria for leading a good and happy life are quite different. The experimental psychologist or physicalist is simply adding the sums of observed behavior and attempting to quantify the results. Yet, they also list what constitutes happiness and the goals of what, in any other context, would be a good and ethical life.

Psychoanalytical theory postulates that we are the sum of all our pathogenic thought process, all of the wrongs that have been done to us, all of the wrongs that we have done to others and the accidents of genetics. Are these not all value judgments based on how people should act towards one another? Is this not a statement that leading a good and ethical life not only leads to your own happiness; it also leads to the happiness of those around you?

In the most abject behaviorist doctrine, the goal is to create a world in which people respect others and act in such a manner as to insure the happiness of their fellow beings. What is the goal in *Walden Two* but an ethical and moral society in which emphasis is placed on helping your fellow beings and eliminating conflict and aggression.

Chapter 8 - Religion and Psychology

When we look at the development of each of the religions that we have reviewed and the development of psychology, there are astonishing similarities in the evolutionary process. Both the religious adherents and psychologists were engaged in a crucial argument concerning the duality of human nature: mind and body, spiritual and material, essence and illusion, and both solved the problem in virtually the same manner – we are the essence of both and both affect the reality we know. Both groups puzzled over how to lead a good and happy life, and both groups came to virtually the same decisions when applied to human behavior:

The evil, dysfunctional acts you commit against others harms both you and the ones upon whom they are inflicted.

To be happy you must feel that you are contributing to others in some form; you must feel part of something greater than your individual existence.

No rewards or reinforcers, no material things can be held in the mind to produce happiness – you are in a way the sum of the good deeds you have accomplished.

Do unto others as you would have them do unto you.

Many conflicts have arisen over the past decades concerning the apparently opposing positions held by religion and the science of psychology. One demands faith and the other demands the absence of all faith. One demands adherence to laws that come from God, and the other states that it holds no laws save those of nature and science. Both have had learned advocates who denounced the beliefs and opinions of the other.

Both groups have fought even greater battles within schisms of their own religion or schools of psychology, than against different religions and different schools of psychology. When these differences are viewed in perspective, however, it is amazing what similar beliefs are held among diverse religions and supposedly opposing schools of psychology.

When we look at the real goals of religion and psychology, we see they reach toward the same possibility, each seeking to teach its followers how to live life to its full potential. There would be no religion and psychology if mankind did not yearn to reach this potential. We would not have investigated something so intensely if our interest were not so amazingly powerful that it has driven us relentlessly to seek the answer. We would not have striven so hard and for so long unless within each of us there is this drive to reach God, or the good and happy life, was not so intense and overriding that it overshadows all else. So many lives have been devoted to answering these questions, and so many lives have been lost in meaningless conflict when each of us holds virtually the same answer to the ultimate question.

This work has shown the mass of data indicating similar answers to the same major questions. Religions and psychology should work together to build a framework in which mankind can reach its potential, rather than concentrating on the elements in opposition; we should be concentrating on the myriad elements held in common. Until we work together to reach these common goals, we will be the less, "for no man is so blind as he who will not see."

Notes

1. *National Survey on Drugs and Health.* (U.S. Department of Health and Human Resources, Substance Abuse and Mental Health Statistics, 2002) p. 20.

2. *National Suicide Statistics 2000.* Center for Disease Control and Prevention, (U.S. Department of Health and Human Resources, National Clearing House, 2002) p. 28.

3. Frederic Spiegelberg, *Living Religions of the World* (New York, Prentice-Hall, 1956) p. 119.

4. Ibid, p. 90.

5. Ibid, p. 92.

6. Ibid, p. 106.

7. Byron Earhart, *Religious Traditions of the World* (Harper Collins, 1990) p. 729.

8. Ibid, p. 741.

9. Ibid, p. 750.

10. Frederic Spielgelberg, *Living Religions of the World* (Prentice-Hall, Inc. 1960) p. 125.

11. Ibid, p. 135.

12. Byron Earhart, *Religious Traditions of the World* (Harper Collins, 1993) p. 752.

13. Ibid, p. 753.

14. Ibid, p. 763.

15. Ibid, p. 74.

16. Ibid, p. 765.

17. Ibid, p. 770.

18. Ibid, p. 772.

19. *Asvaghosa's Life of Buddha. Trans. Samuel Beal* (New York, Colonial Press, 1990) p. 306.

20. Ibid, p. 318.

21. Henry Clarke Warren, *Buddhism in Translation* (Boston, Harvard University Press, 1922) p. 122.

22. Ibid, p. 40.

23. Ibid, 150.

24. Ibid, 152.

25. *Further Dialogues of the Buddha.* Trans from the Majhima Nikaya by Lord Chalmers (London, Oxford University Press, 1926) p. 117.

26. Ibid, p. 123.

27. Henry Clarke Warren, *Buddhism in Translation* (Boston, Harvard University Press, 1922) p. 122.

28. Ibid, p. 122.

29. John B. Noss, *Man's Religions* (London, Collier-Macmillan Limited, 1966) p. 181.

30. Ibid, p. 198.

31. Vincent A Smith, *Asoka, The Buddhist Emperor of India* (Oxford, Clarendon Press, 1920) p. 200.

32. John B. Noss, *Man's Religions* (London, Collier-Macmillan Limited, 1966) p. 209.

33. Ibid, p. 212.

34. Ibid, p. 213.

35. Ibid, p. 217.

36. Ibid, p. 221.

37. Sir Charles Eliot, *Hinduism and Buddhism* (London, Edward Arnold and Company, 1921) p. 30.

38. H. Byron Earhart, *Religious Traditions of the World* (San Francisco, Harper, 1993) p. 496.

39. Ibid, p. 500.

40. Ibid, p. 510.

41. Ibid, p. 521.

42. Ibid, p. 522.

43. Ibid, p. 524.

44. *The New York Public Library Desk Reference* (New York, Simon and Schuster, 1989) p. 190.

45. Robert Watson, *The Great Psychologists* (Philadelphia, J.P. Lippincott, 1978) p. 32.

46. Bertrand Russell, *A History of Western Philosophy* (New York, Simon and Schuster, 1945) p. 3.

47. *The Pre-Socratic Philosophers*, ed. G. S. Kirk (England, Cambridge University Press, 1984) p. 239.

48. Ibid, p. 247.

49. Hippocrates, *De Anima*, chap. II.

50. Bertrand Russell, *History of Western Philosophy* (New York, Simon and Schyusterm 1945) p. 6.

51. Plato, *Phaedo*.

52. Plato, *The Republic*, Bk.IX, p. 571.

53. *The Encyclopedia of Philosophy*, Paul Edwards ed. (New York, Macmillan Publishing Co., 1972) p. 151.

54. Aristotle, *De Memoria* 2, 45 1b, 17.

55. Augustine, *On the Trinity*, Book X, chap. XI.

56. Wilhelm Wundt, *Contributions to the Theory of Sensory Perception* (Leipzig, Engleman, 1897) p. 14.

57. Morton Hunt, *The Story of Psychology* (New York, Doubleday, 1993) p. 172.

58. Ibid, p. 178.

59. Ibid, p. 186.

60. Ibid, p. 198.

61. Ibid, p. 199.

62. Ibid, p. 202.

63. L. S. Hearnshaw, Freud: Man and Scientist (New York, International Universities Press, 1951) p. 17.

64. Morton Hunt, *The Story of Psychology* (New York, Doubleday, 1993) p. 246.

65. Edward Lee Thorndike, *Animal Intelligence* (New York, Macmillan, 1911) p. 38.

66. Morton Hunt, *The Story of Psychology* (New York, Doubleday, 1993) p. 267.

Bibliography

Aristotle. *De Memoria.*

Augustine. *On the Trinity.*

Beal, Samuel, trans. (1900). *Asvaghasa's Life of Buddha.* New York: Colonial Press.

Chalmers, Lord, trans. (1926) *Dialogues of the Buddha from Majjhina Nikaya.* London: Oxford University Press.

Earheart, Bryan H. (1993). *Religious Traditions of the World.* San Francisco: Harper.

Edwards, Paul, ed. (1972). New York: Macmillan.

Eliot, Sir Charles (1921). *Hinduism and Buddhism.* London: Edward Arnold and Company.

Hernshaw, L. S. (1911). *Freud: Man and Scientist.* New York: International University Press.

Hippocrates. *De Anima.*

Hunt, Morton (1993). *The Story of Psychology.* New York: Doubleday.

Kirk, G. S., ed. (1984). *The Presocratics.* England: Cambridge Press.

Noss, John B. (1966). *Man's Religions.* London: Collier-Macmillan Limited.

Plato. *Phaedo.*

Plato. *The Republic*

Russell, Bertrand (1945). *History of Western Philosophy.* New York: Simon and Schuster.

Smith, Vincent, A. (1920) *Asoka, The Buddhist Emperor of India.* Oxford: The Clarendon Press.

Spiegelberg, Frederic. (1956) *Living Religions of the World.* New York: Prentice Hall.

Thorndike, Edward Lee. (1911). *Animal Intelligence.* New York: Macmillan.

Warren, Henry Clark. (1951). *Buddhism in Translation.* Boston: Harvard University Press.

Watson, Robert. (1978). *The Great Psychologists. Philadelphia*: J. P. Lippincourt.

Wundt, Wilhelm. (1897) *Contributions to the Theory of Sensory Perception.* Leipzig: Engleman.